Rooted in Joy

Rooted in Joy

CREATING A CLASSROOM CULTURE OF EQUITY, BELONGING, AND CARE

Deonna Smith

JB JOSSEY-BASS™
A Wiley Brand

Published by John Wiley & Sons, Inc., Hoboken, New Jersey.
Published simultaneously in Canada.

For general information on our other products and services or for technical support, please contact our Customer Care Department within the United States at (800) 762-2974, outside the United States at (317) 572-3993 or fax (317) 572-4002.

Wiley also publishes its books in a variety of electronic formats. Some content that appears in print may not be available in electronic formats. For more information about Wiley products, visit our web site at www.wiley.com.

Library of Congress Cataloging-in-Publication Data:

Names: Smith, Deonna, author.
Title: Rooted in joy : creating a classroom culture of equity, belonging,
   and care / Deonna Smith.
Description: First edition. | Hoboken, New Jersey ; San Francisco : John
   Wiley & Sons, Inc. : Jossey-Bass Publishing, [2023] | Includes index.
Identifiers: LCCN 2023010373 (print) | LCCN 2023010374 (ebook) | ISBN
   9781119898030 (paperback) | ISBN 9781119898047 (adobe pdf) | ISBN
   9781119898054 (epub)
Subjects: LCSH: Educational equalization—United States. |
   Anti-racism—United States. | Classroom environment—United States. |
   Teaching—Social aspects—United States. | Teacher-student
   relationships.
Classification: LCC LC213.2 .S63 2023 (print) | LCC LC213.2 (ebook) | DDC
   371.102/4—dc23/eng/20230503
LC record available at https://lccn.loc.gov/2023010373
LC ebook record available at https://lccn.loc.gov/2023010374

Cover Design: Wiley
Cover images: Flowers:© komunitestock/Getty Images
              Paper Texture: © Silmairel/Getty Images

SKY10053744_082223

This book is dedicated to every teacher who still believes in joy.

To my mother, my biggest cheerleader, my amazing husband, and the rest of my incredibly supportive family.

A special thank you to my support systems at school. The colleagues who have supported me along the way, my mentors, and the people who believed in me and this book.

Most important, this book is for all my students—all the little humans who touched my life. You taught me more than they'll ever know. I love you.

CONTENTS

Rooted in Joy

INTRODUCTION

Not everything that is faced can be changed. But nothing can be changed until it is faced.

—*James Baldwin*

I'm hoping that this is one of those great books that you pick up over and over again. There are many books in my library that I visit when I want to laugh, when I need some inspiration, or when I want to feel I'm not alone. I've tried to include a little bit of all that in this text.

This book needs a spot on your shelf where you can pull it out from time to time and revisit the ideas and concepts. You can pick it up and put it down again as you navigate the ups and downs of the classroom. The reality of teaching is that we don't often get time to invest in ourselves and our craft, but I hope you will take the time to work through this text and reflect on the content and its messages.

I've poured myself into this book. I've included many stories about my time as a teacher—having changed the names of others, of course—because I want you as the reader to know that I see us as accompanying each other on this journey. I've studied anti-racism and teaching for many years, but that doesn't mean that I'm the ultimate authority and expert. I'm learning with you. I wanted to create something that would resonate with teachers and administrators, something that they could see themselves and their students in. I intentionally mix experience with anecdotes, theory, and frameworks. Many of the ideas that I talk about in this book warrant some extra time for study and consideration. Because I couldn't fit everything that I wanted into this text, I instead tried to synthesize and chunk everything so it's clear what you need to know to move forward.

And though this book is primarily written for teachers, it applies to everyone engaged in K–12 schooling. Teachers can't do it alone. We need school and district leaders who are also committed to belonging, care, and joy. In fact, equity work is even more impactful when it's taken on school-wide. So, if you're, say, a school administrator, the mindsets that are detailed here are just as important for you as a leader, and the strategies that you'll find here can be shared with your teachers. Or, if you're a parent or caregiver, this book can give you insight into how you can center joy, belonging, and care at home.

When you visit the following pages, I invite you to do so with an open mind and heart. I invite you to think about the students in your sphere and reflect on your interactions; I'm guessing you'll read something that will remind you of a particular student or incident. And although you might find yourself reflecting on mistakes, I also hope you'll find at least one story that affirms what you're already doing.

As you proceed, take note of the strategies that might transform your classroom(s)—and reject the ones that don't apply to your situation. But more importantly, stay grounded and open minded. Ask yourself what brought you to this profession? What did you hope to accomplish? What expertise do you already bring to the classroom? What more do you need to know?

The truth is, education has perpetuated harm in this country. Our schools and systems have been used against our students. Halls and classrooms have problematized students and made them feel unwelcome. Too many kids struggle through classrooms and leave hating school and hating learning. I'm saddened but not shocked when I hear someone say that they "hated" school. How we experience school affects the rest of our life. Not enough teachers are grappling with this reality. However, I know there are thousands who want to fight for equity, but they might not know how. I hope this book will find its way into the hands of those who really need it. Those who are open to building a healthy and safe classroom ecosystem where all their students can thrive.

But before we dig in, let's get a few questions out of the way.

Why do we need to talk about things like "equity" and "anti-racism"?

Certainly with all the negative press and all the confusion, contention, and flat-out fake news about critical race theory (CRT), anti-racism, and cultural responsiveness, specifically addressing anti-racism and equity could be controversial. So why call it by name?

Because until we face the fact that racism and other systems of oppression have affected education, we can't undo that impact. Unless we are honest about the fact that our educational system was designed to produce inequitable outcomes, we will never experience equity. For example, consider the following.

In Florida, a proposed Advanced Placement course in African American studies was banned because it "lacks educational value" (Mazzei & Hartocollis, 2023).

In 2021, the Texas state senate voted to end the requirement that women's suffrage and civil rights be included in social studies curriculum. The move means that Texas students are no longer required to learn about Susan B. Anthony, Dr. Martin Luther King Jr., or Cesar Chavez—to name just a few (Williams, 2022).

Across the nation, an estimated 2,523 books were banned in schools. Of these, 41% included LGTBQ+ characters or protagonists, 40% included people of color, and more than 30% dealt with issues of racism, activism, and race (Martin, 2022).

From school boards to political debates, the "anti-CRT" movement has been a highly debated topic. In some states, like Iowa and Colorado, districts ask teachers to post all their lesson plans online for approval. Other states have laws that give parents the right to approve or reject lesson plans. The Stop W.O.K.E. Act in Florida—"Wrong to Our Kids and Employees"—heavily regulates how teachers are allowed to even talk about race in their classrooms (Waxman, 2022).

I've even heard of school boards banning anything having to do with the words *diversity*, *equity*, or even *social-emotional health*. This disturbing wave has been called many things, from whitewashing history to fascism.

And it's certainly affecting our classroom cultures.

There are many "-isms" that we face in our classrooms, both interpersonally and institutionally. We have to fight classism, sexism, xenophobia, transphobia, ableism, ageism . . . the list goes on. This book seeks to embrace all intersections of identity, but will specifically focus on race and culture. And yet, the practices can be used to reduce all kinds of inequity in the classroom—to actively work toward an inclusive classroom that honors the diversity of all students.

Is all this just good teaching?

Yes! It is absolutely important that we specifically address the way that racism has affected our classrooms, but you'll notice that many of the strategies in this book are just good teaching practices that will help *all* students thrive.

There will of course be practices, suggestions, and frameworks presented that seek to specifically dismantle the legacy of racism in education. Some teachers may face scrutiny for pursuing asset-based or other equity work. Ideally, teachers wouldn't be persecuted for wanting the best for their students. In fact, equity work is even more impactful when done on a school-wide or district-wide scale. The reality is, in many states and districts this work has become vilified. But, even if you work in an "anti-CRT" state, that does *not* mean that you can't build a joyful, inclusive, and asset-based classroom ecosystem. Ultimately, you're seeking to improve outcomes for yourself *and* your students—you just might need to be strategic about your messaging.

We do need activists and allies who are ready and willing to push back against these harmful laws and book bans. Many teachers across the country are experiencing burnout and/or "compassion fatigue" and don't have the bandwidth to organize against these laws. But, ultimately, we need teachers and their allies to organize for change.

There are so many terms: Black, Brown, BIPOC, and so on. What do they all mean?

Labels and words matter. In this book, I sought to be intentional about word choice when discussing different groups. First, *Black* is capitalized because it refers to a collective history, culture, and racial group. In most contexts I'm talking about Black American students. You'll notice that the term *white* isn't capitalized. Many major publications, such as the *New York Times* and *Wall Street Journal*, don't capitalize *white*. When *white* is capitalized, it's typically associated with white supremacy groups and white nationalists. In an effort to delegitimize those organizations, I am sticking with the lowercase *w* for this book.

But what about the term *Brown*? You've probably heard the phrase *Black and Brown*. So whom does that include? According to Chow (2017), there is no set definition of *Brown*. Many people in the South Asian community refer to themselves as *Brown*. Some Indigenous communities, Southeast Asian, and Latinx communities identify as *Brown*. There does appear to be some dissension in regards to whether East Asian folks are *Brown* (Chow, 2017). But there is no definitive answer. In this book, *Black and Brown* refers to *non-white* people in the United States, a synonym for *people of color*. (The term *BIPOC* stands for Black, Indigenous, [or] people of color.)

It is important at times to be very specific. For example, some data and references will refer specifically to Black students or Indigenous students because, although there is a need for collective solidarity and a coalition between Black and Brown folks, we have different experiences in the US education system. This book will always strive to use the most specific and accepted term by the group referenced. Black and Brown people are not a monolith, and neither are individual ethnic or cultural groups. There might be terms used in this book that do not suit all members, but the intention is never to minimize, reduce, or offend—it is, rather, to find the most commonly agreed-on and updated term.

No doubt in the years to come a new, better, or more appropriate term will arise, and that's good. Language is fluid, and we are constantly in the process of decolonizing and liberating our minds and the ways that we refer to and understand ourselves.

How do things like anti-racism and other equity work interact with other strategies that I'm already using like Class Dojo, Classroom Economy, or Dean's List?

Centering equity and anti-racism is not a strategy. It's an approach and a pedagogical stance. It's what you do in the classroom, but it's also who you are. Being an asset-based teacher doesn't mean that you can only use strategies that are labeled as asset-based. Rather, it means that you operate with a few understandings, such as the following:

- What we do in the classroom matters; in the small interactions and choices that we make we can either enforce or dismantle systems of oppression.
- Systemic racism is pervasive in education, both on a grand scale, like school funding, but also on a small scale, like who gets expelled versus who gets a second chance.
- You'll have to commit to this work holistically. It's not a switch that you can turn on and off but rather a mindset that you need to adopt. Let it grow with you and help you be a better and more intentional educator.

Teachers develop toolboxes and strategies to cultivate classroom cultures and respond to student needs. These come from many places: our credentialing programs, professional development, or the other teachers. When you adopt an equity mindset and approach, you may very well still use many of those tools.

You might find that some of your tools and strategies no longer serve you and your students. There is no checklist that says what's asset-based, equitable, or not. The more you learn, the more you'll be able to see what systems, practices, and tricks move you closer toward an equitable classroom—and which ones move you further away from it.

Many practices in our classroom are informed by carceral practices and ways of thinking. Because of this, many common practices that teachers employ are not equitable, and end up perpetuating -isms like racism or sexism.

When you start to build a healthy classroom ecosystem, you'll want to critically interrogate those harmful practices and adopt new ones that are centered on belonging and care.

Is anti-racism for Black and Brown folks, white folks, or both?

Black and Brown folks have personal experience with racism, but that doesn't mean that we—I'm using *we* because I'm including myself—don't need to understand asset-based and equity work. Racism isn't just about individual actions and attitudes, so Black and Brown people can unintentionally perpetuate harm and racism simply by reinforcing the systems around them. That's because the status quo—what's normal and accepted—is deeply rooted in racism.

White folks need to be deeply engaged in asset-based and equity work, and not just because they want to "help." It is imperative that white folks recognize that in a society where racism thrives we are all harmed. As long as there is one system of oppression, others thrive and build on each other. Our collective liberation must be the goal.

Racism harms everyone. In the classroom, policies that are rooted in inequity or racism harm all students, even white ones. Let's say all your students are white; maybe you're thinking that perhaps that means you don't need to engage in this work. But remember: students learn about how to "be" in school. They receive messages about right and wrong, society, relationships, and just about being human in general. Because your students, regardless of their race, will have to learn to navigate racism and all the other -isms in this world, they need to start learning as soon as possible, and that includes white students.

This book is for Black, Brown and white teachers. All teachers. You might notice that there is quite a bit of advice and time spent on strategies that are more geared toward white teachers. This is because in the United States there are simply more white teachers; according to the National Center for Education Statistics (2020), almost 80% of teachers are white. But the strategies and tips in this book are applicable to everyone.

Will this book help me master behavior and classroom management?

Spoiler alert: a huge component of behavior management is letting go of the idea that all behavior needs to be "managed." This framing is problematic, and I'll discuss it in Chapter 3. It is not the intention of this book to make you a manager. A successful teacher is not one who goes about the classroom managing and responding to every behavior that they don't like or that doesn't align with a cookie-cutter view of what classrooms could look like.

The trouble is that that's what many of us understand classroom culture as being: management—so we talk about "classroom management." The goal, however, is to move away from this thinking and start talking about things like culture, belonging, and joy. This book will help you along your journey of evolving out of that mindset. If you want to be asset-based and equitable, and you want to create a culture of inclusion in the classroom, this book will help you do just that. But it's not an easy fix. It'll be work, and it'll require some mindset shifts. But it is possible.

Before we jump in, just a few disclaimers.

You'll have to give something up. If you want something to change, you'll have to do something different. When you start to see the classroom and the world differently, and start to view the world with an equity lens, your mindset will change and so will your practices. If the classroom ecosystem is to be truly rooted in joy, any practices, policies, and even your own behaviors that don't facilitate joyful, caring, and inclusive communities will need to be retired. Maybe it's a reward system that you've always used, or a book you've always taught. Recently many teachers have moved away from Dr. Seuss because of his long and well-documented history of racism. You might have very fond memories of using Dr. Seuss or even reading him as a child—you can honor those memories *and* let your teaching practice evolve at the same time. It might not be easy, but it's so very worth it. Know that it's okay to do things differently than you always have.

No one book can solve the entire education crisis. In the wake of the COVID-19 pandemic, which in many ways is still an ongoing crisis, an unprecedented wave of truly extreme student behavior has swept through classrooms, putting both teachers and students in danger. This book is in no way suggesting that teachers can single-handedly eradicate or are responsible for these issues. This book is about daily challenges in classroom culture and student behavior. We will certainly explore de-escalation strategies, but there are some behaviors that are too severe for teachers to face alone.

The practices and approaches in this book work best when coupled with school leaders who are committed to both students and teachers. Additionally, these strategies will be even more meaningful in districts that sufficiently fund schools so they have all the resources they need. Policies that limit teachers' ability to meet the needs of their students undermine the frameworks in this book.

Even if you don't feel supported by your school leader or your district, you can still find great value in this text. The practices in this book are designed to help you create a flourishing classroom ecosystem, despite the significant system-wide challenges educators are facing.

So here's where we're headed. In Chapter 1 I'll start with talking about who we are, and what we bring to the classroom as individuals. Then, in Chapter 2, I'll talk all about asset pedagogies and how to develop an asset-based lens.

Chapter 3 is hefty. There are all sorts of ways that we need to shift our thinking if we're going to be able to effect real change. So I've broken them all down into bite-size portions and grouped them by themes. I encourage you to take your time with them; don't overwhelm yourself with too much at once.

Chapter 4 is where we start building a healthy ecosystem. We'll talk about laying the foundation for the classroom culture. Then Chapter 5 is all about maintenance—how to keep your healthy classroom ecosystem thriving.

Along the way, I share stories from my teacher days, research-based practices, frameworks, and everything in between. And, you might notice, there's some repetition in here; some things bear repeating!

Let's jump in.

"Education can't save us, we have to save education."

—Bettina L. Love, *We Want to Do More Than Survive: Abolitionist Teaching and the Pursuit of Educational Freedom*

CHAPTER 1

When We Know Better, We Do Better

I grew up in a well-meaning very homogenous town in Washington state, where I struggled to navigate an education system that just wasn't designed for students like me: Black, low-income, and first-generation college-bound. With hard work and a lot of luck, I got a bachelor's in political science, Spanish, and international studies and then a master's in education. I started teaching 5th grade in Oakland, California, working with who some would call "challenging" and "urban" students. But this was not like what you often see on TV and on social media; the students in the "tough" neighborhoods were bright, creative, and hilarious! Working in underfunded schools and with students that the education system had all but given up on catalyzed my passion for educational justice.

It was during this time that I began to cultivate and refine my skills as an educator. My vision was simple: focus on relationships, have an "asset" mindset, and always see education as liberation. Before long, opportunities to coach and support other teachers presented themselves, and I eventually became an administrator. The social justice (re)awakening of 2020 crystalized my understanding of my true calling: walking with teachers and other stakeholders through this work. In 2022, I officially became Dr. Smith and started working with even more schools and teachers across the country.

This story has a happy ending, but there were many bumps along the way. There were days, weeks, and months where I thought I just wasn't cut out for this. I made so many mistakes. Like many teachers, I started my career out confused, trying a hodgepodge of everything I had seen online and learned in my credentialing program. I spent weekends drowning in a pile of grading and lesson plans. I shed many a tear out of frustration and exhaustion as I reflected on how chaotic my classroom was. Looking back, I have so much more understanding and grace for myself. I know now it's okay to have days filled with doubt.

Slowly but surely, I built up my toolbox. Having the right tools is essential, but more than that, it's important to have the right mindset. The internal work, unpacking your own identity, mindset, and even mental health, has to be the foundation. Ultimately, it starts with you. But that doesn't mean that you're going at this alone.

Teachers can do it (but they can't do it alone).

Search through Teachers Pay Teachers, an online teacher resource hub (https://www.teacherspayteachers.com), attend a conference, or go to a PD (professional development) session and you'll find dozens of solutions for behavior management. Classroom economies, tokens, apps—you name it. So how come so many of them don't work?

At the end of the day, many of those systems could work, but they don't include the heart work and mindset shifts that teachers might need to make in order to be highly effective. And so anytime I launch a program or training I always start with the teacher. That's because any curriculum, program, or approach is only as culturally responsive, or "asset-based," as the teacher implementing it.

But don't fall into the dangerous pitfall of blaming teachers. Politicians, social media, and even some families are all too quick to point to teachers as the problem—instead of listening to them for the solution.

Retention and recruitment have been significant challenges in education, and it's easy to see why. Many teachers are simply underpaid and just have too much on their plate. To top it off, they're being held solely responsible for every problem in the classroom.

It's easy to get caught in a cycle of frustration. We can describe all the reasons why teachers need more support, why we need more admin to step up, what the district could do differently. We should all be advocating for those changes and continuing to highlight systemic barriers to student success.

We can't self-care our way out of toxic systems, and we can't relationship build our way out of a toxic school culture. The most pervasive and persistent inequities in education cannot be solved within the wall of one classroom.

But for our students to thrive, we need to embrace a both/and. We need *both* systemic change *and* to shake up the way we do things in the classroom. Teachers *do* have agency!

If you're a teacher, start to think of the classroom as its own little ecosystem: a semi-autonomous zone where you can reimagine what joy, accountability, and community can look like! Finding your agency and owning your power and influence in the classroom will lead to better outcomes for your students—but it will also help you reconnect to the joy of teaching.

Note: this book can't replace a supportive administrator or a well-resourced school district, but it can help teachers who want to figure out how to build a community rooted in joy despite the barriers and challenges both teachers and students face.

A NOTE ON SHAME

Teachers are under intense and heightened scrutiny at every turn. Despite being charged with a near impossible task, respect and trust in teachers in the United States is low. Several states have laws that give parents the right to contest and oversee what goes on in the classroom. Families being involved can actually be incredibly beneficial for students, but that involvement shouldn't translate to the right to unilaterally veto lesson plans. In some states teachers are required to submit lesson plans to the district for review ahead of time to ensure that they aren't teaching "critical race theory." Disrespect like this puts teachers and the entire profession on the defensive.

When I first started learning more about researched-based practices and social justice in education, I felt waves of shame. Shame because in the early stages of my career I made most of the mistakes that I'll talk about in this book. I focused on punishments, perpetuated systems of harm, and didn't do what was best for my students. It was difficult to learn that maybe I wasn't as effective as I thought I was. The great Maya Angelou said, "when you know better, do better." Once I started learning how to be a better teacher, I had to be mindful to not let my shame take over. That shame can put you back on the defensive. Though it's true that in my first years as a teacher I didn't have a prep, subs, sick days, or support, and all of these things certainly affected my ability to be the best teacher I could be, I had to be honest with myself and look inward. I had some agency over my classroom, and there were things that I could have done differently. I acknowledged those feelings of shame, but then I moved on. I focused on giving myself grace and doing better.

Talking about issues of race, equity, and social justice can also bring on feelings of shame. It's true that the legacy of racism, sexism, homophobia, and all other forms of oppression in this country is shameful. Learning about it and grappling with it can bring up many different feelings, but shame just isn't helpful.

Here's what prolific researcher and professor Brené Brown has to say about shame (in a 2012 TED talk): "If you put shame in a petri dish, it needs three ingredients to grow exponentially: secrecy, silence, and judgment. If you put the same amount of shame in the petri dish and douse it with empathy, it can't survive."

Again, when you lean into shame, you go on the defensive, refusing to look inward. Don't rob yourself of an opportunity to learn and reflect. Notice when you are feeling defensive or ashamed. Let that feeling come without judgment of yourself. Then start to make room for grace and moving forward.

YOU *SHOULD* SEE COLOR

My white teachers were amazing. They were highly qualified, well-trained, veteran teachers—some of the best. But they weren't the best teachers for *me*. I grew up in a world where it was cool to be color-blind; the phase of the decade was "I don't care if you're black, white, or purple." And I get the sentiment—my teachers believed that it shouldn't matter that I was a little Black girl in a very white school. But the thing is, it really did. It mattered that my family and I inherited a 400-year legacy of oppression. It mattered in many ways, but here are a few.

It mattered because I grew up in a Black neighborhood where the schools were underfunded. Because of this my parents lied about our address to get my sister and me into a better school, so in essence we "stole" our public education. I don't know if I would have been able to accomplish what I have today without that school and fake address. And this story is not unusual—I've known countless other people who did the same thing. For families who are savvy and have the capacity, they get their kids into the "better" schools. But this story would have been very different if my family didn't have the resources to actually get me to school every day. Even in large districts where there are numerous "high-performing" charter schools, or they use an "open enrollment" system where students aren't bound by the address, you still have to consider the logistics of getting your kids to and from school each day. You'll need reliable public transportation or a car, and a lot of time.

When I worked in the Bay Area, I had students who drove in 45 minutes to an hour each way into school every day. The schools were in historically Black, Brown, or working class neighborhoods and were pretty good options. But the families had been priced out of their homes. They couldn't afford to live where the safe and well-resourced schools were—or even in their old neighborhoods, for that matter—because of gentrification and the housing crisis. Color-blind teachers miss all this. They miss that many Black and Brown folks don't have the option to be color-blind.

It mattered because I never saw myself in the curriculum, books, or adults around me at my school. There were no Black teachers or even staff members. I didn't know where I fit in. I felt alienated as a child—I felt loyal to my roots and heritage as a young Black woman, but also ashamed because I didn't fit in to the world around me. There were only a few books with Black protagonists in our school library: *Roll of Thunder, Hear My Cry* and *Amazing Grace*. I checked them out over and over, searching for belonging. We didn't learn about Black excellence, joy, or Black history. We only discussed Blackness as it related to whiteness: slavery and civil rights— after which my teachers insisted racism had ended.

It mattered because the kids and students didn't understand what it meant to be Black and different—from my hair that didn't blow in the wind like theirs, to my lunches that didn't look like what the other kids brought each day. I fielded questions every day relating to the fact that I was the first (and sometimes last) Black person that my peers interacted with. Their only frame of reference were the Black people on TV like Dave Chappell and the "gangster rappers" in music videos. Remember, this was long before Black Disney princesses and a Wakanda Forever section in the toy aisle. They asked why I didn't like to dance, and why I wasn't loud like all the stereotypes that they consumed. My white teachers had no idea how to handle situations like this.

These are just a few reasons why when my teachers said they "didn't see color," the effect was that I was invisible. Everything about me was very much Black. The other kids treated me like I was Black. Their steadfast attempts to sanitize me of my Blackness further alienated me from my own self-image and identity. It was not intentional, but it was still very much harmful.

My teachers did a great job with me academically, but they didn't know how to be culturally responsive. The fact is, the school was designed to fit the needs of the white students, and it did that very well. I learned to adapt in a process called *code-switching*.

Code-switching is a linguistics term often associated with alternating speaking different languages or dialects in the same conversation. But more recently the term has become associated with adjusting one's behaviors in order to assimilate, or fit, in to a dominant culture. For my behavior to be accepted, I had to code-switch.

What does that look like? It's different for all cultures, but here's my example.

I came from a very expressive culture and a high-energy environment. My family was communal, collective, and group oriented. This did not always align well with the very narrow expectations of what it meant to be a "good" student. I would rather work in a group, but so much in school is focused on individual assessment. "Working quietly" didn't mean that I was more productive—in fact, it was the opposite. Songs, routines, and interactive play was how I learned best, when I was expected to "sit and get" it was incredibly difficult for me meet that expectation. Even though I went to a Montessori school, which tends to be more open, I still had to leave my culture at the door.

My culture didn't really have a place in my classroom. The cultural values and ways of being that I grew up with were penalized in that classroom. While the white students only had to learn the material, I also had to learn how to survive (let alone thrive) in a classroom where the norm was based on being able-bodied, neurotypical, and white.

I'm not trying to inspire sympathy. I learned how to navigate the school system. I learned all the rules and expectations frontwards and backwards. In the Black community, we have a saying that you have to work twice as hard to get half as far. I deeply internalized this sentiment and put in the work.

But the reality is, I shouldn't have had to. And so many students like me didn't have the same advantages: kids whose parents didn't lie about their addresses or would have but weren't able to drive them to a farther school. Kids whose life situation was problematic enough in any number of ways that they didn't have the internal resources to learn how to navigate the white system.

So, we need to do better. But before we can do better we have to be willing to grow.

INTENT VERSUS IMPACT

In the DEI (diversity, equity, and inclusion) and asset-based world we talk a lot about intent versus impact. It's critical to understand intent versus impact in education because teachers are some of the most well-meaning people on the planet. Most—if not all—go into the profession with generous intent: to help and support kids. Unfortunately, sometimes their impact can be quite the opposite.

Intent is how you think and feel; it's who you are and what your goals, desires, and wants are in any particular situation. It's the impetus underlying all your actions.

Impact is the effect of your actions. It's what others experienced in response to your actions—how your actions land.

What can be tricky is accepting accountability for our intentions *and* our impact. Just because I didn't mean to harm someone doesn't mean I didn't. And just because we intend to have an inclusive and equitable classroom doesn't mean we actually do.

It can be very hard to own our impact. When I first started teaching I worked with many veteran teachers who thought of equity work as an add-on—something that they talked about in one or two PDs a year and then got back to pedagogy. So I tried to help them see how important this work is. My intent was to offer support to help teachers meet the diverse needs of their students—and then hoped that in turn they could help me with my areas of weakness. My intent was to get them to understand that equity work isn't a fad; our kids' *lives* were at stake.

But my impact didn't match my intent. I unintentionally frustrated teachers. I wanted them to feel called in or called on, but instead they felt called out. I inadvertently made them feel shame—and when folks feel shame they shut down.

So I had to find a way to convey some seemingly contradictory truths:

- This work is important and urgent.
- This work can be uncomfortable.

- We want people to feel they have agency—because they do.
- We don't think in terms of blame; we believe that when we know better, we can do better.

I find the comparison of intent and impact extremely helpful when working with students as well. It means that you can still address a situation where harm has occurred with nuance rather than with just assigning blame.

For example, here's an issue with academic integrity that I had to address when I was a dean. A typically very high-performing student who was experiencing upheaval at home copied another student's book report almost word for word and submitted it to her own ELA teacher, thinking that the two teachers wouldn't notice. Well, they noticed—and it was impossible to know who copied whom because the work was very good and on par with what we'd come to expect from both students. And because of a district policy that we had to enforce, both students were supposed to be punished: each would fail the class and miss out on all the grade-level activities.

By explaining the concepts of intent versus impact, we were able to get the student who had copied the paper to come forward and explain that the other student had had no idea. She had established a reputation as a high-performing student and she hadn't wanted to lose that, but her mental health was in a bad place and she wasn't able to get to all her assignments. She explained that her intent had been only to find a way to skirt by—that she never intended to hurt anyone else. Fortunately, we were able to have that discussion and start to heal and repair the situation.

In brief: if when reflecting on your teaching practice you find moments when your intent didn't align with your impact, acknowledge that fact—accept it and take accountability—but don't get stuck in shame. Instead, take to heart the lessons in this book (and elsewhere) so that you can be more mindful in the future. The internal work starts with you owning and understanding your impact.

Lenses and Mirrors

In his 2022 book *The Four Pivots: Reimagining Justice, Reimagining Ourselves,* Shawn Ginwright explains the difference between lenses and mirrors. When we engage in equity work, we often talk about using a "social-justice lens" or an asset-based lens. When we do this we think critically about the world around us. If you're using an asset-based lens, you'd examine

(continued)

a system as if for the first time and actively consider how anti-racism, for example, permeates that system. (The same is true for other approaches—we can reexamine practices and policies with a feminist lens or an ableist lens.)

This is very much an external process. We look at the ails of society and problem-solve from the perspective of the outside looking in, hoping to pinpoint in what ways external systems and factors are harming our students.

What we must also consider is a mirror. When we reflect and look in the mirror, we're (hopefully) able to see the ways that we unintentionally perpetuate these systems as well. That means taking a hard look at our insecurities, biases, challenges, and shortcomings.

Once you start it, this mirror work is an ongoing process. Ideally, you'll come back to this mirror work again and again. Each time you reflect, you'll probably notice something different. Try not to become overwhelmed and paralyzed by this work. We're not assigning blame here. We're just trying to learn and grow. Once we know better, we can do better.

THE INTERNAL WORK

If we learned anything in the wake of the social justice revolution of 2020 it's that we all have some unlearning to do. And that starts with internal work.

Perhaps you've heard about unconscious and implicit bias. We won't go into it too much, but it's important to understand that bias and our personal areas of growth affect how we show up for our kids. We all have a culture and a frame of reference, and bias lives within that.

Bias shows up *big* time in how we address behavior. What are your ideas about students moving around while you're talking? What about lateness? Or noise level? How you respond to these behaviors is related to bias because our culture informs us on how we're supposed to behave.

A behavior that particularly irks me is when students are disrespectful—specifically being dismissive or not addressing elder adults—like students that don't speak to their grandparents or mock older people just for being older. This was a huge trigger for me—and that comes from my cultural frame of reference. In my family, when older people walk into the room, you acknowledge them. "Respect your elders" is a value that was drilled into me. So when I witnessed a student use profanity and speak dismissively to their grandparent at a conference I was shocked! And I reacted very strongly. Later, I had to step back and think about why I'd been so triggered—and to consider all the ways my cultural frame of reference informs how I teach.

The internal work isn't linear and it isn't easy. It means that you have to examine the many levels of culture. To help you in your process with this, I've developed a number of reflection questions to help you understand more about your culture, background, and biases—and how you can mitigate them. You'll find those online at www.wiley.com/go/rootedinjoy.

And, again, I urge you to try to stay open-minded and not judge yourself. This is not a paradigm for blame, and it's not a paradigm for shame. That's because this work is never "done." We are all still learning and growing in this journey. It's just like with teaching: taking our initial credentialing program is just the beginning. There's a great deal more to be learned on every day after that.

Project Implicit

I'm not the only one telling you that there's no shame in holding biases, implicit or otherwise. We all frame our worldview through more than one lens. As a means of demonstrating just how prevalent and pervasive biases are, the team at Project Implicit offers a series of free, securely encrypted online tests—Implicit Association Tests (IAT)—that anyone can take to get a clearer picture of their own mindsets. According to their website: "The IAT measures the strength of associations between concepts (e.g., black people, gay people) and evaluations (e.g., good, bad) or stereotypes (e.g., athletic, clumsy)." The tests concern such topics as age, disability, gender, race, religion, sexuality, skin tone, and weight. Check them out at https://implicit.harvard.edu/implicit/takeatest.html.

WHAT HAPPENS IN THE TEACHERS' LOUNGE STAYS IN THE TEACHERS' LOUNGE

I've long believed that the connections we make with other teachers on our staff can be the difference between quitting and staying. That's because teaching is such an intense, immersive, and highly specialized career. When we bond with other teachers we experience that "oh, wow, they really get me" feeling—which can make all the difference.

As a teacher and an administrator, I spent time and resources to make the teachers' lounge a fun place to be. I was the teacher that always brought baked goods, cleaned the spills that no one would take responsibility for, and kept the space decorated according to the season. I have a profound belief in the teachers' lounge—but unfortunately it's not all sunshine and positivity.

The truth is, just like student culture, adult culture can become toxic. Teachers are perennially overworked, under-resourced, and just spread too thin—and all teachers respond to this pressure differently. Some teachers isolate in their rooms and need time alone to regroup or readjust. Other teachers flock to the lounge to spend time either bonding with other teachers or venting, which can be very cathartic.

Once I was visiting a school in Marin County and the teachers were speaking openly about a "rough" family that had attended the school for a few years. The school was mostly white, plus a few Black families and a small community of Salvadorian students. One of the Black families had six kids with the oldest in 8th grade; at this point, every teacher in the school had had at least one of the Greene kids. The parents had quite a reputation for being "difficult" to work with.

In the teachers' lounge they were "comparing battle scars." The eldest boy had thrown a chair. The youngest girl apparently spat on a substitute in kindergarten. Then the conversation started to take a turn.

Why didn't the parents take school seriously? The Greene kids didn't have any discipline, they didn't value school, they were just disrespectful. They were learning it from the music that they listen to, the TV shows that their parents let them watch, the neighborhood that they lived in . . .

Individually, none of these teachers would think of themselves as racist, but they fell victim to what can happen when teachers dehumanize their students and get too caught up in venting. Venting turned to first thinly veiled and then downright racist comments. In that particular situation, I turned to one of my favorite strategies: questioning. How do you know they don't value school? Have you had conversations with the parents about their values? What type of shows? What neighborhood? When people are forced to confront and explain their racist beliefs, it gives them an opportunity to reflect and think critically about them.

So what do we do? We need to make space for teachers to share challenges and triumphs, but also not in ways that degrade students and families. And when teachers talk about behavior it's very easy to slip into this type of conversation. The stress of responding to big behavioral concerns and the perception of being in a "judgment-free zone" can result in us not always displaying our best selves.

In the same way that we seek to build positive classroom cultures, administrators and teachers alike need to be cognizant of the adult culture at the school. And that culture must also be rooted in anti-racism if the classroom cultures are to be successful.

So, how do we start to build this culture?

We start small. When you hear problematic comments about students or families, speak up. (Perhaps say, "I hear you. I also think there's a more constructive way to frame this problem.") If a colleague is frustrated and their venting turns to degrading or dehumanizing the student, speak up. ("I understand you're upset. And, I have to admit, I'm uncomfortable hearing students talked about that way.") And try to keep your tone calm, not sharp. Remember, we don't want to shame anyone; we just want to call folks into the conversation. Keep in mind you can always start with curiosity. When I hear things like "they" or "those kinds of people" or "that community" I'll simply start by asking the speaker to clarify their comments. Providing a moment for reflection can go far.

Some schools ask teachers to "debrief" or share their experience with the future teacher at the end of the year to help them get to know their incoming students. There are certainly some benefits to this; I remember making my seating chart based on the feedback of the teacher from the year before. But such conversations can also elicit inappropriate comments, which can turn toxic.

Sometimes what students need most is a fresh start, a teacher to look at them without the assumptions of the past. If teachers debrief with each other in advance, kids can't get a truly clean slate. It's a bit like why scientists often conduct double-blind experiments—because it's all too easy to influence behavior even unconsciously.

So, my first recommendation is to just let the students start with a clean slate. Or, if you must chat about the kids in your previous classes, focus on their assets and their strengths.

TEACHER SELF CHECK-IN

The energy that you bring to interactions with your students matters. A regulated adult could pull a child from a burning building without emotional harm. A dysregulated adult could traumatize a student with a scraped knee.

I've had the pleasure of observing and working with teachers around the country. I've always been struck by how impactful a teacher's mindset coming into an interaction can be. Two teachers could have vastly different reactions to the exact same behavior depending on their individual backgrounds, their cultural biases, and where they are at emotionally. Consider the following scenario:

> Let's say one of your most challenging students is having a tough day. They've been ignoring you all day, not completing any work, and refusing to participate. This isn't the first time that this student has acted this way. Maybe you asked for support but no one was available. You have no preps today. It's only 10:00. You're not sure what to do, so you're thinking about threatening to take away recess, just to get some control back.

I have personally been in this situation at least 100 times. On days when I am well—meaning, I'm coming to the situation regulated, as my best teacher self—I don't end up shouting, "If you do that one more time I'm taking your recess!" or "Last warning before I call home!"

On days when I am not well, when I'm dysregulated, not only would I likely shout and threaten the student, I might also end up crying on my lunch break—or at least when I get home. In frustration I might Google "best careers for former teachers." What's worse is I'll probably be so upset that it'll be difficult to give my challenging students a fresh start—even on the next day.

Emotion

In my work, when I ask teachers where they are at emotionally when they're responding to student behavior, they're usually in one of two states.

Teachers who respond from the *emotional* space are often hyper-focused on their own emotions and the emotional state of the student exhibiting behaviors. It's important to understand antecedents in behavior, recognize patterns, and contextualize the student experience. However, it can be problematic when teachers do this without also dealing with the impact that their students have on *others*. Teachers who jump to only analyzing challenging behaviors often fail to respect boundaries—their own boundaries and/or the boundaries of the other students, misbehaving or otherwise. The most well-meaning teachers can easily fall into this trap.

Teachers in this state are wrapped up in how they are feeling: scared, sad, or frustrated. They can't step outside of their emotional state. Alternatively, these teachers are too wrapped up in their students' emotions. they are fixated on how the student is feeling, so much so that they can't start responding.

Now, it's okay if the first place you go to when responding to a student is how they are feeling. It's better to start with over-sympathizing than with dehumanizing, but know that this can't be the last stop. When you're responding to student behavior, it's in the student's best interest to be taught how to comprehend accountability and the impact of their actions in a developmentally appropriate way. Teachers in this emotionally sympathizing space might ignore behaviors so as to avoid dealing out consequences. But consequences help kids learn about the impact of their behaviors; kids can't learn if they never experience logical consequences.

Escalation

Escalation might be the space that I encounter most frequently, and it's no surprise. Teachers are already grappling with the big-picture issues in education, and we all have personal ups and downs on top of that. When teachers respond from a place of escalation, it's bad for both them and the student. You might notice your heart rate going up or you might get flushed.

When we hit the escalation zone, we have a physical reaction. The amygdala, the area of the brain that processes emotion, sends stress signals to the hypothalamus. Because the hypothalamus is the brain's control center, it'll tell the rest of the body that it's in distress (Harvard Health, 2020). Once that fire alarm goes off, we might get stuck there for the entire day. Our bodies might go into fight, flight, or freeze mode.

This is when we start handing out threats, ultimatums, and allowing our frustration to take over. We simply cannot do our best thinking when we're escalated; an escalated adult cannot de-escalate an escalated child.

WELLNESS AND WHOLENESS

Fortunately, we have better options!

Wellness

Some teachers are able to respond from a place of wellness. Teachers who have engaged in the internal work of unpacking their biases and starting to think about culture and identity bring a remarkable level of intention to their classrooms. They are also mindful about maintaining their own social emotional wellness. Teachers who are well are able to avoid snap reactions. Their bodies still react to stress—that's a natural and inevitable occurrence—but well teachers know what to do when that happens. They know when they need to step back, take a break, and revisit an issue when they've had a chance to regulate their emotions. And they're in a much better position to help de-escalate a student.

Note, however, that well teachers might still fall into punishment mode. Well teachers understand the systemic oppression, trauma, identity, and other aspects of equity work. But understanding these things doesn't mean we'll always be able to respond from a place of understanding in the moment.

Wholeness

Wholeness is the ideal space for both students and teachers. Wholeness is different than wellness because in a state of wholeness you recognize the full humanity of both you and your student. Not only do you understand boundaries, inequity, trauma, and healing but also you've found a way to incorporate these concepts into your teaching practice. You're able to respond to your students in a way that meets their emotional needs, and you also understand how as a loving and caring adult you can create learning opportunities and teachable moments for them. And because you see your own full humanity, you're able to get your own nervous system back on track. You give yourself grace, while holding both yourself and your student accountable for what happens next. You set boundaries for yourself, and help other students set boundaries as well.

It won't surprise you to hear that a sense of wholeness can only come after reflection and internal work. When you have a sense of wholeness, you're able to see the big picture of the school day, week, month, and even year. Think about wholeness as all the pieces coming together—as those days when you're just "on." This doesn't mean that everything outside of the classroom is going perfectly; it means that you've tapped into your own sense of agency.

Note that these states are absolutely not stagnant. There are days when you'll be feeling whole and days when you'll be feeling escalated. There is no shame in being in either of these spaces. What we are looking for here is *awareness*. It is powerful to be able to step back and recognize that you're reacting from a place of emotion at the moment. The ability to recognize and name your emotions helps you get your agency back in real time. It helps you move between phases, and it breeds a deeper understanding of self.

WHEN IT'S TIME TO HEAL

I didn't really understand collective trauma, and that an entire school could be dealing with it, until I became an administrator. I had seen teachers struggle individually with their personal lives or with difficult students—but, indeed, an entire building can have trauma. Until that trauma is healed and dealt with, moving forward is very difficult if not impossible.

When I stepped into a particular school—let's call it Marigold Elementary—I thought I knew what I was getting in to. I knew that the staff members had had quite a few rough years with behavior and discipline. They had some students who would frequently leave the classroom and roam the halls. They had a few "tantrum" students who would tear things off the walls and destroy materials. I knew that neither the teachers nor the administrators really knew how to deal with the high-needs population the school was designed to serve. There was distrust, bureaucracy, and tension among school leaders, teachers, and district personnel. Caught in the middle of all this were hundreds of Black and Brown kids trying to learn.

When I became a school leader I promised myself that I would never forget what it meant to be a teacher in the day-to-day. I refused to let myself forget about the unique joys and challenges of classroom life. I thought that, because I had a plan to specifically focus on adult culture and teacher wellness, rooted in the teacher experience, I could be the person to lead the school out of this rough patch. I was wrong.

Marigold had a few years of poor leadership, undertrained teachers, and a district that was very checklist oriented—the kind that gave teachers hour after hour of paperwork to fill out but very little support, development, or coaching. As a school leader team, we made some much-needed and big changes to the way things were done. I was excited to start putting the teacher's feedback in action and get the school back on track.

What I failed to realize was that sometimes changing things up is just not enough. The teachers absolutely wanted things to change at the school. They liked the additional support, the pancakes in the break room, the feedback channels—but they weren't fully able to appreciate all the shifts that we made. All the great new things that we were doing could not erase the previous five years of poor leadership, the students who'd destroy classrooms and be ignored, the endless busywork from the district, and the observations that made the teachers feel policed rather than supported. The teachers of Marigold had not healed.

You might have experienced this for yourself. When harm happens in our communities, of course we want to see improved and different outcomes—but before the changes can really be internalized we first must heal.

I had noticed that, no matter how many of the teachers' suggestions I implemented, no matter how hard I worked to ensure that they felt cared for and seen, my support was not landing with them. This brought me so much frustration, but looking back I can see my mistake. As a leader, it was my job to meet the team where they were at. If I could go back, I would strive to funnel the energy I spent feeling frustrated into hosting more circles, making more space—even bringing in counselors so that teachers had a chance to process what they experienced.

So, what does this mean for teachers? Recognize that, sometimes, you might need to heal. When you feel yourself perpetually responding from a place of emotion or escalation, that's a clear sign that you might need to take a step back and process what you've been experiencing. If you don't take the time to heal, you won't be able to fully accept, acknowledge, or bring about any changes in your school community.

How can you get there? A trained professional—such as a licensed psychotherapist—is the best person to help you along your healing journey. But even if you don't have access to one, you can still find roads to healing. Maybe the first ideal road is one that literally leads you out of town for a retreat where you can unplug—you can create your own retreat with a staycation as well. Maybe it starts with creating a space for yourself at home that you can turn to whenever you need it. Finding a support group can work wonders. Even starting up a new hobby that has nothing to do with teaching can help you find a path to heal from the trauma you've experienced in the classroom.

This will look different for everyone, but take the time and space to heal.

SELF-CARE, COMMUNITY CARE, AND SUSTAINABILITY

Self-care is ubiquitous in education discourse because teachers need it. In fact, it might be the only thing keeping teachers in the classroom, because responding to big student behaviors and addressing major behavior concerns is a common reason for teachers to leave the profession altogether. Schools have a vested interest in making sure teachers tend to their self-care—so why are they so bad at making it happen?

One of the challenges is that self-care has been relegated to bubble baths and yoga classes. As wonderful and absolutely necessary as those are, that's not all that self-care is. Self-care should make teaching more sustainable. It should mean happier kids and happier teachers.

What we can't forget about are the systemic forces that are making it quite literally impossible for teachers to care for themselves. If teachers are feeling unsupported in the classroom, are working hours over their contracted time, and are emotionally drained day after day, all the bubble baths in the world won't help.

School-Based Barriers to Self-Care for Teachers

➤ Poor management meeting time
➤ Repeated reduction of planning or prep time
➤ Lack of or unclear communication
➤ Exhaustive busywork or nonessential tasks
➤ Increased accountability or expectations from school and district leaders that is not coupled with increased support

---

But if we can reframe the way we think about behavior and classroom communities, it would free up the mental space and energy we need to care for ourselves. So we—ourselves and our education communities—need to do two things at once. Teachers must take the individual responsibility to prioritize their own self-care, and school leaders and administrators must acknowledge the practices and policies that serve as barriers to that self-care, because otherwise that self-care may not be sustainable. (I'll return to this angle in a bit.)

Self-care doesn't stand alone; I recommend teachers also consider and invest in community care. Is your school community healthy? A toxic school culture can permeate into the adult culture and make each day feel like a marathon—and each school term a life sentence.

So, how do we invest in community care? When you start to cultivate the classroom ecosystem, you'll no doubt (in time) help students understand that they need to be kind and courteous to have healthy relationships with each other. There's no better way to model that than with the adult culture. Students absolutely notice how the adults in the building interact and treat each other. As you start to freedom dream and imagine what the classroom will look like and feel like—which we'll do in Chapter 4—extend those dreams to the adult culture. How will the adults show that they love each other and care for one another?

SEEING THE WHOLE PICTURE

Two seemingly opposite ideas can absolutely be true at the same time (Figure 1.1). Teachers are underappreciated and overworked. The education field can feel unsustainable. Many school districts claim they're concerned about teacher well-being, but then they enact and perpetuate policies and practices that are detrimental. And we need to address all that.

What's also true is that teachers have a unique opportunity and responsibility to build classroom communities that help their students thrive. The job doesn't always align well with this goal, but that doesn't make it any less important.

When I've talked about this work with teachers, I've gotten a lot of pushback about "one more thing": "We can't handle doing even one more thing as teachers; we're already exhausted."

In no way am I minimizing the fact that this work takes effort and intentionality. It's also true that we want our students to thrive. Making that happen does involve a learning curve—perhaps a steep one—but the benefit of creating a healthy classroom ecosystem far outweighs the initial cost. Ultimately, there's an added bonus and benefit: healthy classroom ecosystems mean less work and frustration for teachers, thereby making teaching more sustainable, not less.

The key to is give yourself some grace. Be patient with yourself along this journey. We can get there together.

Figure 1.1 Seeing the Whole Picture

Seeing the Whole Picture

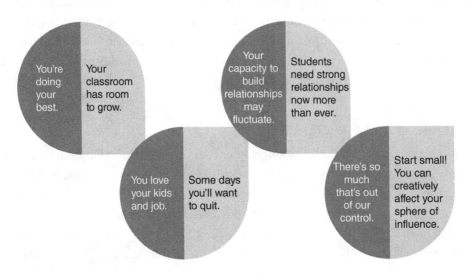

Give Yourself Some Grace!

CHAPTER 2

What We Need to Know

In May 2020, the world cracked wide open. The murder of George Floyd set off a chain reaction that led to an overdue reckoning on race in the United States and across the world. Summer 2020 saw the largest social justice movement in US history, which led to a reexamining of almost every system that holds our society together (Buchanan & Bui, 2020). Although most of the scrutiny was focused on the criminal (in)justice system, education was also well overdue for an audit.

These problems weren't new, and this isn't the first time scholars have discussed the systemic racism in public education. But this moment in particular brought much needed attention to the so-called achievement gap, the disproportionate penalization of Black and Brown kids in school, the overrepresentation of white women in the field of teaching, and so much more.

Unfortunately, the activism was met with an equally swift wave of resentment, racism, and bigotry. School boards across the country passed measures about "identity politics" and critical race theory, a term that many misunderstand. This has culminated in some dire consequences for teachers, students, and the future. In some states, there are laws on record that prohibit teachers from even talking about systemic racism, as well as from supporting their LGBTQ+ students. Trans students, who already face transphobia in their daily lives, now must also contend with what can only be understood as persecution in schools (Human Rights Council, 2022).

As a result, some schools are running away from words such as *anti-racism* and *equity*—and others are doubling down on their efforts to help their students thrive. The entire concept of anti-racism has become highly politicized, and the terminology itself can seem like alphabet soup. So it's important to understand the terms, what they all mean, and why we need them.

ANTI-RACISM AND ASSET PEDAGOGIES

Anti-racism and *anti-bias*, as they pertain to education, are part of a larger pedagogical approach that is sometimes comprehensively referred to as *asset pedagogies*. There are many asset pedagogies, but the unifying concept is that we see our students from an asset lens. According to the National Education Association (2021), asset pedagogies focus on the unique strengths that our students bring to the classroom. Teachers viewing a student through an asset lens means they don't focus on all the ways a student doesn't measure up to schooling standards, and they don't view students' particular cultures and experiences as something the students need to overcome. That's because culture, race, ethnicity, and other identity markers are not the barriers to students' success—systemic oppression is. Teachers who use this approach strive to help their students connect with their unique brilliance.

This mindset requires some critical divergent thinking. This is because pretty much everything about how our school systems were designed sets us up to look at kids from the perspective of deficit: How do they measure up to the standard? What standards are they not meeting? What expectations are they not reaching? An asset-based approach refuses to focus on standardized metrics as a way to assign value.

Before *anti-racism* and *anti-bias* entered the dominant culture lexicon, teachers were often talking about *culturally responsive* and *culturally relevant pedagogies*. Let's briefly explore the history and importance of these terms.

In the 1994 first edition of *The Dreamkeepers*, Gloria Ladson-Billings challenged teachers and school leaders to adopt a truly culturally relevant pedagogical practice. The book specifically looked at highly effective practices that teachers were using to help their Black students thrive—by unlocking the power of culturally relevant pedagogy, or CRP, which has three essential pillars. The first pillar is academic achievement, meaning that we have to recognize that the pedagogical practices we've employed in the classroom have been leaving some kids, primarily BIPOC kids, behind. The second pillar is cultural competence, meaning that teachers need to understand the cultural context that students bring to the classroom. The third pillar is sociopolitical consciousness, meaning that teachers have to recognize the systemic and societal challenges that students are facing (Ladson-Billings, 2009). Sociopolitical consciousness affects every sphere of the classroom, including behavior. Think about what our students see on the news and experience every day; they bring that along with them into the classroom, and it can show up in how they behave.

Culturally sustaining pedagogy (CSP) expands on CRP and highlights that not only do teachers need to recognize the culture of their students but also that schools should be a place where culture lives, thrives, and is sustained (Paris & Alim, 2017). It is no secret that education has been used to remove students' culture. Both the United States and Canada have a long and shameful legacy of physically removing Indigenous folks from their communities and placing them in boarding schools. In these schools they were stripped of their language, cultural aesthetics, and practices. The goal was to steep them in the dominant North American culture instead.

History has shown us how schools and education can be used to strip culture, but can they also be places where it's sustained? CSP sees the opportunity for schools to be where students can not only feel validated in their identity but also where they can learn more about their culture and cultivate their identity. Some schools might offer opportunities for students to learn more about their cultures, for example, during heritage months and ethnic studies classes; however, in CSP, culture is not just an add-on, but rather a central component of the pedagogical approach.

Abolitionist teaching draws on CRP and other asset pedagogy ancestors, but adds more layers and concepts for teachers and school leaders to grapple with. In *We Want to Do More Than Survive*, Bettina Love describes what she calls the "educational survival complex," which sets some kids up to fail because the systems are intentionally designed so that not all children can thrive. The achievement gap is perpetuated because schools are not designed to be spaces where specifically Black and Brown students can succeed, either academically or emotionally. Even schools that boast "high test scores" or "college-readiness" do so at the expense of their students' emotional wellness. Getting students college-ready, especially those who have been systemically denied access, means getting your students to comply with the dominant culture as quickly as possible. Schools are not joyful liberatory spaces, but rather mechanism for students to be stripped of much of their culture and individuality. By pushing back on standardization and conformity, abolitionist teachers make space for other experiences, such as joy, creativity, and identity (Love, 2019).

Anti-racist teaching draws on intellectual legacy of these approaches and many more asset pedagogies, but it also specifically grapples with the systemic racism in education. Although all of your students may or may not be directly affected by systemic racism, it's existence is a threat to us all. As long as the policies and practices in place threaten one group, all groups are in danger.

Consider this definition of *anti-racism* from the NAC: the "active process of identifying and eliminating racism by changing systems, organizational structures, policies and practices and attitudes, so that power is redistributed and shared equitably." We can see that being anti-racist is much more than thinking racism is bad.

What does this look like from a pedagogical perspective? If you identify racism in schools, that means that you are calling out policies and practices that are rooted in racism. If you are eliminating racism, not only are you calling out these policies but also you are working to actively push back against them. Organizational structures can be difficult to tear down on your own, but it starts with recognizing and voicing concerns about inequity. It might not be readily obvious that an organizational structure is based on racism but with a closer look it can become clear. Consider, for example, schools that have policies that prohibit students from using their native languages. Initially they thought they were "helping" students by forcing them to speak

English because there is a sense of urgency to build English language fluency, but that policy clearly rejects the assets that bilingual students bring to the classroom. Polices that seem to make sense academically can absolutely be rooted in racism.

Attitudes can be the most challenging to disrupt, and they show up consistently in behavior. Whether or not teachers are aware of it, we all hold unconscious biases that are informed by racism, and those beliefs impact our students (Chin et al., 2020). One study estimated that teachers make more than 1,500 decisions a day. With that much overwhelm, your brain develops shortcuts to process what's happening around you. Unfortunately, those shortcuts are rooted in biases, even if you would consciously never act that way.

Consider this study conducted by Stanford in 2015. Teachers were given different discipline records for students. Some names suggested that the students were Black such as Deshawn and Darnell. Other names were more likely to belong to white students Kyle or Greg. The researchers found that the teachers were actually more likely to assign harsher punishments to the students that they assumed were Black (Okonofua & Ederhardt, 2015). Note, these are teachers that would not *consciously* identify as racist or bias—which just highlights the power of the subconscious mind.

Teachers are not immune to racist images, ideas, and perspectives in the media. Teachers are just people, so when they're in front of a classroom, they bring all those biases from their outside life and experiences.

Asset pedagogies aren't just about your attitudes, they're also about your actions. If you're in education long enough, you'll see the pendulum swings of reform. There are always new ideas, new policies, and new initiatives. We've seen No Child Left Behind, Race to the Top, Common Core, and so many more just in the last 20 years. Despite the persistent nature of reform we cannot become desensitized to the anti-CRT policies that have sprung up since 2020. Even teachers in "safe" states, where these policies are not being voted in, need to be actively engaged in the fight against them.

When you adopt an asset pedagogy lens, you'll start looking at practices, pedagogy, and even politics differently. You'll want to make changes and shifts in the way your run the classroom and, hopefully, even the way you live your life!

INEQUITY BY DESIGN

A classroom is only as culturally responsive or equity-focused as the teacher leading it. For this work to be meaningful and impactful, it has to become who you are, not just the books you read or the podcasts you listen to. Unfortunately, there are no handy checklists that you can cross off.

This work requires you to change your mindset, your lens, and look at yourself in the mirror—often.

Often times teachers will want a ready-made solution or framework. This book will certainly give you a set of tools, mindsets, and practices, but it won't help you or your students unless the tools are accompanied with reflection and the internal work. Because there is a persistent myth that we should "just teach" and that somehow curriculums and classrooms can be apolitical or agnostic of societal norms and values, it's easy to fall on the side of "objectivity." If you just teach what's in your teacher edition and follow the rules, you'll be neutral. That is not the case.

Let's just take classroom rules or expectations for example. When I first started teaching, flexible seating wasn't a common option for students. It was just assumed that everyone would sit in their assigned chairs during instruction and that was that. There wasn't consideration for neurodivergent students or collaborative learners, or even student whose bodies didn't fit comfortably in the standardized chairs. That expectation, that everyone sits quietly, was not objective; in fact, it was tailored to a very specific kind of student.

We are conditioned to think of our classrooms as neutral or objective spaces, but that isn't the case. Some teachers want to avoid teaching about topics related to race and inequity to seem objective. However the act of deciding whose stories get told, and whose history deserves to be studied, is in no way objective. Once we realize that the standard vision of a classroom isn't objective, it can be easier to understand why we must push for a diversity of thought and ways of being. If you come to this work, thinking that you just have to get your Black and Brown students to work inside a "normal" classroom, you will be unsuccessful. The goal is not to just find a box of gimmicks and tricks to get your Black and Brown students to comply with a system that was in many ways not designed for them. Instead we orient ourselves toward doing the deep, internal work necessary to design spaces rooted in joy, belonging, and care, that liberate our students' potential.

If you find yourself frustrated by the pervasive and persistent nature of inequity in education, you might start to feel like the system sets up our kids to fail, and you're right. Part of what makes asset pedagogies difficult to implement is that they are contrary to the nature of how schools were designed to function. Unfortunately, inequity isn't an accident.

Let's go back in time, all the way to Horace Mann and the "common school." In the 19th century, when it was decided that kids should be going to school (and not working in factories) schools taught the three "Rs: reading, writing, and arithmetic. The United States had a burgeoning immigrant population, and along with the basic subjects schools were a way to transmit and acculturate newcomers into the "American way." Early schools employed the banking model of education where students were empty silos, ready to be filled with knowledge from the teachers. Students went to school, sat in rows, and education was mostly direct instruction. At that time, if a student was not following directions teachers would use corporal punishment (Marshall, 2012)!

The sit-and-get model of instruction did not meet the needs of neurodivergent students or encourage students to thrive in school. For students who weren't part of the dominant culture, school was where they learned the values, morals, and behaviors of the hegemonic culture. Schools didn't have to be culturally relevant because they were focused on forcing everyone to fit one cultural mold.

Schools have seen plenty of reform since then, but we are still dealing with the vestiges of this system today. Even the idea that students all develop at the exact same time in yearly intervals forces children to fit into a very narrow box. If a student deviates from that, perhaps they develop at a different pace than "normal," that student is penalized.

Can we be surprised then that now our students are struggling? The system that we force our students into is not designed to help them thrive. The system is also set up to ensure that some students fail. Some schools focus on remediation and others focus on college readiness; there are a finite amount of AP seats in our classrooms and only a fraction of college graduates will make it to and through college.

ALLOWING YOURSELF TO DREAM

There's so much out there about what doesn't work in our classrooms, but what kind of classroom would we want?

It's a simple, yet critical question.

When we start to create our classroom we have all kinds of ideas and hopes and dreams. We get excited, but then we get bogged down by reality.

The truth is, the type of classroom that we want, the completely idealized version, probably won't happen tomorrow or next year. That's the thing about this work. It's not necessarily immediate, but that doesn't make it any less important.

That means that it's not always best to get caught up in what-ifs. What if it doesn't work, what if the district says no, what if my principal doesn't support it? Don't start there.

Start with the dream, whether it's realistic or not, and work backwards from there.

When I work with teachers, I encourage them to think about it as sowing seeds. The prayer of Oscar Romero, a revered Jesuit priest, reads, "We plant the seeds that will one day grow. . . . We are prophets of a future not our own." Oscar Romero fought for peace in El Salvador, but died before he was able to see all his work come to fruition. Let's look at instruction to illustrate this metaphor more vividly. When you're a kindergarten or 1st-grade teacher, you spend much of you time teaching your students to read. You'll give them the tools and building blocks like phonemic awareness and letter sounds. They won't exactly be reading Shakespeare but it's incredibly important work. These are the seeds. Then, one day, when they are in their Honors English class, reading *Twelfth Night* out loud, or they'll recognize a vowel team in *King Lear*, it'll be because of their very first teachers.

It's the same with building the classroom community. The day after you try an ice breaker or a team builder, you won't come to a classroom of peaceful students singing kumbaya together. But maybe a few weeks later, with time and consistency, something will just click.

So dream big. Don't let the limitations of our current reality rob you of something better.

Dreaming *can* be difficult when you're in the trenches because we often have to be pragmatic. When I was a first year teacher, I struggled with the reality I *wanted* for my kids, and the reality that my kids would actually be stepping into. I used to ask myself all the time, am I preparing them for the real world? In the real world, you won't get credit for late work and when you get to college you'll have a ton of reading to do. In the real world if you're distracting your coworkers, you'll get fired. I was consumed with this idea of the "real world" until I heard a speech by Sir Kenneth Robinson.

Sir Kenneth Robinson, well-regarded education scholar, has given many speeches about the myth that we must focus on preparing students. Once I had the pleasure of seeing him speak about education in person. He shared a story that has stuck with me since. He was walking into an open house and saw a sign that boldly declared, COLLEGE STARTS IN KINDERGARTEN. His response was, "Sorry, no, it doesn't." He urged us to think about what we lose when we focus so much on the real world that we forget about the very real children in front of us. Instead he suggests that we focus on letting kindergarten be kindergarten, a place to learn, play, and explore. There's nothing wrong with wanting your kindergartener to go to college one day, and college access is an equity issue, but perhaps we are focusing so much on the real world that we aren't allowing kids to be kids.

His story hit home for me. I didn't feel like I could just be a kid when I was in school. My teachers were always tough on me, whether they meant to be or not. I didn't have a Black teachers, nor Brown teacher in K–12. Because the majority of my white teachers were not culturally responsive they were tough on me in the sense that they expected me to conform to the dominant culture. There wasn't much space for me to bring my Blackness into the classroom. They didn't think about the fact that I came from a different side of town, that my family struggled with systemic racism and poverty, or the fact that I was a first-generation college-bound student. They wanted me to succeed, and they thought that the path to success for me was following the exact footsteps of my white classmates.

My teachers were tough on me because they expected me to code-switch and adopt the cultural values that were in their frame of reference. There was no road map for me; my family was very culturally Black and my school was very culturally white. I had to learn to navigate both worlds and be the intercessor between the school and my family. When I got to college, I knew the stakes were even higher. There was no college fund for me to fall back on. I was also an undiagnosed dyslexic and ADHD, but we couldn't afford extra support or tutors. My margin of error was very slim if I wanted to get into college. When I saw other white kids breaking rules and laws, I knew that wouldn't be an option for me because my parents had no sway or resources to get me out of trouble. Again, this isn't a sad story. I made it through, I got a full-ride scholarship to get my bachelor's and eventually my master's and doctorate. But when I reflect on my own experience of schooling, I see that I was never able to just be a kid because I was so focused on walking a path to success that was actually designed for me to fail.

When I became a teacher, I thought I'd be well equipped to help my students on the same path. When I was in the classroom I saw so much of myself in my Black and Brown students. I had so much empathy for them as they patiently explained things to their parents, signed their own forms, and struggled to find a place for their identity and culture. Because I saw myself in them, I thought it was my job to make sure they were ready for what they might face.

It was something of tough love. I wanted to get them ready, especially my Black and Brown girls. The world would be so hard on them, and I felt it was my duty to expose them and get them ready for reality. If I had high expectations and no room for error now, they'd be prepared for it later when a white teacher or a teacher who didn't understand cultural relevance did as well. If I was strict about using "proper" grammar, then when they were in high school adults would call them "well-spoken" and treat them with respect instead of making assumptions about their intellect because of their use of African American vernacular English.

What I failed to realize was that two things can be very much true at the same time. Kids will face a very unjust world and they do need to be ready for that. But what's also true is I have the unique opportunity to cultivate a classroom environment where Black lives matter, neurodivergence is "exceptional," speaking Spanish at home is an asset, and praying five times a day is "cool."

Why do we need to replicate and reproduce the harmful systems of the outside world inside our classrooms? We can very much prepare our students and set them up for success without having to murder their spirits and teach them to leave their cultures at the door. I've seen many teachers of color may be drawn to this method. Because we know just how hard it can be, we want to be extra hard on our students. I've also seen female teachers being unintentionally harder on their female students as a way of preparing them for a very misogynistic world. These behaviors come from good intentions, but they do not allow for classrooms rooted in joy.

This is why I don't encourage teachers to set up classroom economies or other strategies that boast "real-world" application. Do they work? Yeah, sometimes they do. Do they teach kids about money management and responsibility? Also maybe. I thought about using these practices after seeing many teachers share their success with them on social media. But I had to take a step back. There was just something a little sad about a 2nd grader paying rent for their desk every week to learn about the "real world." My ideal classroom prepares students for the world, without necessarily reproducing systems that cause so much harm. I want them to focus on being in community with each other, not if they have enough tokens or rent their desks.

It can be tempting to make sure that you are transferring life lessons to our students. In a way, that is our job. When I work with teachers, they are often concerned about what will happen to their students in the future if they don't teach them discipline, time management, and responsibility.

This is a valid concern. Teachers who work with older students especially can find themselves frustrated with what they perceive as a lack of preparation from previous teachers. This happens quite a bit with middle school. Teachers always tell me what kids "should" have learned or "should" be able to do. Surely if you've been attending school for 8 years and you're 13 years old, you should have some emotional regulation skills or you should know not to talk over someone when they are speaking. But getting caught up in this "should" game isn't productive for teachers or students. When you're too busy thinking about what students should be able to do, you don't have time to dream about the possibilities of your current reality with them.

I was working with a teacher who actually taught in my hometown of Spokane, Washington. She wanted to be sure that she was getting her 6th graders ready for middle school, which starts in 7th grade in her district. She gave them quite a bit of homework, sat them in rows, and didn't let them go to the bathroom because they had to do that on "their time, not her time." Toward April and May she'd remind them daily that they needed to be ready, they'd have six or more teachers and they wouldn't be looking out for them personally. I understood her thought process. But when we both sat and reflected on her year, we saw kids that were so focused on getting ready that they had no time to enjoy that last year of having a close relationship with one teacher. Her concerns were coming from a good place, but in reality, the students could have been more prepared perhaps by having another year to explore their identities, build relationship skills, and feel confident in their ability to be successful in school. In fact, many of the middle school teachers were actually moving toward classrooms that focused more on joy and collaboration anyway! The next time it was time to plan for the year, she instead thought about what a transition classroom would look like, one where kids would start to feel prepared for the future but honor where they were at in the present. We discussed how preparation might actually look like discussions about community, empathy, and equity.

There's also something to be said for being developmentally appropriate. Ultimately, our kindergarteners might be students in a 200-person lecture hall in college. Does that mean we should start "preparing" them now be doing phonics lecture style? The reason why students have increasing responsibility is because as they get older they are able to handle more. Remember, their brains are very much still developing! But two things can be true. Any teacher who has taught a class since 2020 will tell you that our students' capacity, attention span, and social skill levels have changed. We can face these new challenges in a developmentally appropriate way *and* still enable our students to experience joy.

When you start to dream about the classroom ecosystem, allow yourself to go beyond just preparing students and academics, and rather see them in their full humanity.

ON HUMANIZING OUR STUDENTS

Do we see our students in their full humanity? Before you jump to answer, take a moment to reflect and consider the question deeply. What does it look like to see the fullness of our students within stringent and oppressive confines of the school day? In most schools, every child has to be exactly where they are "supposed" to be—learn to read at the same time, mature and grow at the same pace—but is that what it means to be fully human?

How do we see the full humanity of our students in the whirlwind that is the school day? There's a lot that you miss when you're in the whirlwind. About two years into my teaching career, I realized that the whirlwind was actually preventing me from being effective. It was just a few days before break, and I had a few extra students in my class that day. The first school I worked at was so underfunded that when a teacher was out, we didn't get a sub. Instead the kids were divided up among the teachers that were at work that day. So on this day I had my regular 5th graders and six extra 3rd graders. It was late in the day, and a student that I had struggled with all year, Johnny, was especially challenging this day. To be honest it seemed like Johnny was acting up for no reason. I was so mad. Definitely responding from a place of escalation. Why was he challenging me? Couldn't he see that there were extra students in the class?

I had even given all my students a pep talk in our community meeting in the morning. I had peppered in all the ice breakers. I really thought I had set myself up for success. When Johnny began to escalate I was on high alert. The younger students were looking to my 5th graders to set the tone. I told them that despite having visitors, we still had a lot to get done that day. Before long, Johnny started off with just playful shenanigans, avoiding work, talking over other students, and roaming about the classroom. That was just the beginning. As the day went on the behaviors got worse. In my brain I always divided behaviors in to two groups: when you're a distraction to yourself or when you're a distraction to others. Distractions to yourself I can handle passively, when you start distracting others, I have to start being more involved. Johnny had entered the second category. My stress level was skyrocketing. At this point I was just trying to get through the day. I had so many fun ideas for the afternoon, little buddy activities with the 3rd graders. I was getting sad and frustrated that I wouldn't be able to do everything I planned. It got worse. Johnny decided to start walking around the classroom, taking supplies from other students, and talking to the 3rd graders while they were trying to do their workbooks. I had given warnings, taken away points, asked nicely, invited him to try a new strategy, basically all the little tricks and tips to no avail.

I asked him to sit back down; he did not. I gave warnings, which turned to threats and before long I was breaking one of my own rules—getting into a very public power struggle with a student. *Spoiler alert: I lost.*

I was yelling, I was heated, I was embarrassed. Why on this day? He knew better! He knew that we were so close to a break, that I had way too many students in this little classroom, that it was almost the end of the day? My choices were limited, we didn't have the culture to send kids to the office. I had already taken away recess.

This is one of the most dangerous positions for a teacher to be in: when you've taken away everything that you can, when you can't call for reinforcements, when you're escalated, and so is the student. My coworker and I used to call this point when "we are out of carrots, and we are out of sticks."

Looking back on that moment, I can see all my mistakes. I didn't de-escalate myself. I just kept getting angrier and angrier. I didn't take a moment to step back and humanize my student. He just became my enemy in that moment.

What does it mean to be fully human as a student? It means that your teacher rejects the dominant narratives of classroom management that relies so heavily on control and instead leans in to the fullness of the human experience. Yes my student was acting unhinged at that moment, but I wasn't seeing him, I only saw behaviors. I saw papers flying, time wasted, and lessons disrupted, but I didn't see a little boy, only nine years old, who did feel like he wasn't being heard. Johnny was never taught how to deal with his emotions. He wasn't yet ready to conform to the stringent and narrow expectations of "good" behavior in my classroom because he was so emotionally dysregulated.

What I saw:

- Anger
- Frustration

- Disrespect
- A problem

What I failed to see:

- A little kid, anxious about the instability at home
- A nine-year-old nervous about spending a week away from the school that offered him meals and routine
- A boy who thrived on consistency now in a classroom with six additional high-needs kids
- A person

So here's what I would have done differently—and please note that there are plenty of proactive things that I could have done to not allow my student to get to that point:

- I could have taken a deep breath, centered myself, and really looked at my student. Even a slight change in demeanor could have done a lot to stop the situation from getting out of hand.
- I could have allowed the other students in the room to have some extra recess time so my student didn't feel quite so exposed when we were talking.
- I could have said, "Right now it seems like we're both upset; I'll address these behaviors with you later."
- I could have shifted to a mindfulness moment for us all to get our emotions in check.
- I could have said, "Let's take a break and do our five senses breaths." When a student is escalated we name five things we can see, four things we can touch, three things we can hear, two things we can smell, and one thing we'd like to taste. Then we take five more deep breaths.

The list goes on . . .

All of that doesn't mean that Johnny didn't get a consequence, or that I wasn't holding him accountable. Because I had already said it, he did stay in for recess. If I hadn't taken away recess, I would have had him work in a different area, clean up the mess that he made, and given him some space to cool down and regulate himself.

In these moments, teachers have the opportunity to either continue to perpetuate a system of harm and dehumanization or push best for their students and themselves.

I didn't make the best choice in that moment, but now I understand without the fundamental understanding that my students are humans first, I can't have a successful classroom culture.

A key mistake that I made was not taking time to de-escalate myself. An escalated adult cannot de-escalate an escalated child.

Think about when you're in the heat of the moment, and the bell is about to ring, and you have to finish a lesson, and your most challenging student is escalated.

You're feeling stressed and your blood pressure is rising because maybe you're already behind and your other students are starting to get agitated.

You're remembering some of the training that you've gone through and you know that de-escalation is the way to go, but when we talk about de-escalation, we are assuming that the teacher or adult themselves is in a position to hold space for the student in that moment. The reality is, that's not always the case.

You might not be in a position to de-escalate if any of the following are true:

- You feel your heart rate increasing (or another physical indicator of stress).
- You're feeling triggered by the student's behavior.
- You're feeling pressed for time or have a strong sense of urgency.
- You're at the last straw with this particular student.

Emotions are normal and healthy, but I was responding to the student from a space of escalation. If I had taken some time, I could have entered a space of wellness or even wholeness.

It can be incredibly helpful for our students to see us working through our emotions and navigating them. In high-intensity moments with your students, you may want to de-escalate yourself before continuing to try and respond to your student's needs.

WHAT'S ALREADY OUT THERE

Take a second to think about all the philosophies of classroom and behavior management that you know. There are token-style strategies where teachers assign points, tickets, or some kind of metric in exchange for something. Maybe the student gets access to a toy chest, extra recess, a homework coupon—some kind of external reward.

There are PBIS-style systems (positive behavioral interventions and supports), where there is less focus on negative behaviors and instead students are rewarded for being positive examples to others and are given clear and direct expectations.

There are apps and programs like Dean's List, ClassDojo, or other monitoring apps that can be as simple as documentation or be a part of a larger school-wide system.

Unfortunately there are still schools using highly punitive measures, such as skipping recess, detention, Saturday school, or kicking kids out of class.

The truth is, many of these programs may eventually work in the classroom. Some teachers might find success with simple or punitive systems. In one of my early years of teaching I used a point system and took away recess and it absolutely worked. I was actually known around the school for having good management, but it certainly wasn't humanizing, culturally responsive, or even remotely anti-racist.

Remember, it's not just about what works, because tokens, fear, and punishments may work for some teachers. Recently schools have even brought back corporal punishment because it "works."

I worked at a school that was incredibly strict and, from my vantage point, oppressive. The school was 100% students of color and a "high-performing" charter school. Unfortunately, it was held up as a model for other schools to follow because of the academic data. It's true that our students were outperforming the local public schools, but the academic data didn't tell the whole story.

There were happy teachers and students from time to time, but overall the school was a joyless place. We had some very carceral practices and rules. Students weren't allowed to talk in the hallway or move an inch out of line. They walked in perfect rows with arms at their sides. They had 30 minutes of play time per day and then it was back to business in class. What was perhaps the most disturbing was that they weren't able to talk to each other at lunch. They sat silently in their seats chewing for 25 minutes each before heading out to the small playground. What was even crazier was that other schools would come and visit and actually praise the order, structures, and systems! To adults, this is what a well-run school looked like.

When teachers raised concerns, the response was "it's working." If we let kids talk, they'll get riled up and won't be able to get back to focusing in class. If they aren't marching like little soldiers in the hall, they'll distract the kids that are in class. Now I understand that there are absolutely practical and pragmatic concerns. It's okay for things to be orderly and structured, but this school looked more like a jail than a place where kids learned.

This worked but at what cost? Is it worth it to snuff out the creativity, excitement, and joy that is absolutely natural in children? For fear that they'll be too loud at lunch?

Before you adopt a strategy that works, ask yourself what metrics you're using to decide if something works or not. If the metric is kids are quiet, conform, easily controlled, and obedient, then there are actually quite a few programs that could work. If your metric is that you build a community, a joyful space where kids are allowed to be the fullest and most authentic versions of themselves, while also being respectful and safe around one another, then you might need to be more critical of the strategies you're using.

Our goal is that the classroom is run well, but that it's also a joyful, liberatory community where all students feel like they have a place.

When you do the internal work, you reflect on your culture, background, and biases. This is nothing to be ashamed about! The worst thing that you can do is run away from your biases and get wrapped up in shame. Any program or training that I do I always start with the participant: the teacher or the adult.

For these systems to work—not that kids are just compliant but rather that teachers are leading classroom spaces rooted in joy, belonging, and care—both practices and mindsets must shift.

In Chapter 3, we'll explore the mindset shifts that will enable you to build a classroom ecosystem rooted in joy, belonging, and care.

CHAPTER 3

Mindset Bootcamp

Here is where we explore some of the inner work that will set you up for building a classroom ecosystem rooted in joy, belonging, and care. The items are organized in five groups. The first two include mindset shifts that apply more to the individual classroom: awareness (The Humanity of These Little Humans) and approaches you might try (Classroom Ecosystems). Following that are the bigger topics of rethinking the concepts of classroom management and evolving from punishment into awareness of consequence—and then mindset shifts concerning equity/racism/social justice and some important truths about trauma.

THE HUMANITY OF THESE LITTLE HUMANS

We must see our students in their full humanity, as people—but at the same time remember that, developmentally, kids just don't understand things like adults do. Of course, kids are often much more observant and teachable than we sometimes give them credit for, but you just can't expect a child to have the rational behavior of an experienced adult.

Mindset Shift 1: Kids Aren't Little Adults

It sounds simple, but when you're deep in the (dis)organized chaos of the school year, it can be easy to lose sight of this concept. Once when I was doing a week-long coaching stint at a school in California, I witnessed a veteran teacher help a novice teacher grapple with this concept. A few very frustrated 1st-grade teachers were eating lunch together while I was warming up some leftovers. Almost in tears, the newest teacher shared about her terrible day: she'd been so excited to do this read-aloud activity but she'd had to pause several times to remind her students to stay in their squares on the carpet. She'd done everything right: they'd practiced the procedures over and over, she'd launched the first read-aloud with clear expectations and practice, and the kids even had a carpet song! Because it wasn't the beginning of the year, she was shocked that this was still an issue. Before I could hop in, the veteran teacher looked at her and said, "Well, Andrea, they're *six*."

It was so simple but so important. Even our oldest students are still teenagers—and we all know about the decision-making capacity of a teenager!

We have to be okay with our kids being kids. No matter how capable they are, their brains are not yet fully developed. In fact, school should serve as a safe place for them to make bad decisions and learn how to navigate responsible decision-making.

If you find yourself in a frustrated, at-your-wit's-end moment, take a breath, step back, and remember that they're just kids.

Mindset Shift 2: Assume Best Intentions

"Assume best intentions" sounds quite simple, but in the heat of the moment it can be quite difficult. What does it really mean to assume best intentions? It means that when you perceive your student's behavior, let your first thought and reaction be curiosity. Instead of jumping into frustration, exasperation, and anger, first check in with yourself, asking these questions:

- What am I bringing to the interaction?
- What emotions am I feeling?
- What assumptions am I making about this situation?
- Am I responding from a place of emotion, escalation, wellness, or wholeness?

This helps to humanize your students and yourself.

If you have a student who requires quite a bit of behavior support, you can fall into a pattern and jump to assuming that their behavior is more of the same, thinking the worst. When I worked at a school briefly in Indiana during my student teaching, one of the veteran teachers, Ms. Hyde, had a student, Aiden, who really got under her skin. At the time I described them as "oil and water." She said he "irked" her. And he did. It was clear in all their interactions that there was just something about him that bothered her. After several weeks, and lots of threats and ultimatums, it seemed like teacher and student were finally working in the right direction.

Ms. Hyde was raising funds for the students to go on a field trip by selling Candygrams, and the money was kept in her desk. She had been teaching for many years and had never felt the need to lock the desk. Then one day, the money went missing. None of the students gave the teachers any information about who it might have been. But Ms. Hyde "knew" right away that it was Aiden. It fit perfectly into his existing pattern of behavior. Even more condemning, he was in her classroom after school on the afternoon it went missing. And Ms. Hyde wasn't secretive about her suspicions; she told Aiden outright that she knew he'd done it. Ms. Hyde wanted Aiden suspended or even expelled right away, but our principal wanted to take some time to do a proper investigation. In one of her more problematic rants in the teacher's lounge, Ms. Hyde referenced the mostly Latinx neighborhood Aiden lived in and the "culture of crime" he was "soaking up."

When the dust settled and we got to the bottom of it, it turned out it was actually one of the girls in a different class, Melinda. The teacher down the hall had sent Melinda to get the pattern blocks from Ms. Hyde's room. Melinda said she saw an opportunity—the money was sitting right there in the desk—and she took it. But for Aiden, the damage had already been done, and their relationship never recovered. Ms. Hyde apologized, but Aiden's behavior spiraled even more. He made inappropriate jokes about her regularly and refused to do any work in her class.

I don't know if Aiden would have ever been the type of student that never needed any redirection, but what progress they had made was shattered when Ms. Hyde so openly accused him. A few years later I learned that Aiden had been expelled the next year after having similar behaviors with a different teacher. I can't help but think: Did Aiden internalize what Ms. Hyde had said? Was that the last straw for him?

As adults we walk the line between knowing what to expect and anticipate from our students and giving them fresh starts. Behavior can certainly be cumulative, and it's important to keep track of how students are progressing, but students can sense when you're assuming the best of them and when you're assuming the worst.

If teachers don't assume best intentions, they can cause irreparable damage—both to the students and within themselves.

Mindset Shift 3: Behavior Is Feedback

Behavior doesn't happen in a vacuum. When students talk out of turn, refuse to go to their desks, or elope, which in the context of many schools means leaving the classroom or even the building without permission or supervision, they are responding to something. The stimuli that they are responding to may be in their head or at their desk, but they are always responding to something.

When I was teaching math, I had a student who was constantly disruptive. It was a challenge every day to get through the lesson. And every day it was something new. A toy under the desk, talking out of turn, getting up and bothering other students, coming in late . . . at a low point he was just shouting random rap lyrics while I was explaining ratios.

I tried all of the tactics: sticker systems, calling home, no recess—the list goes on. One particularly frustrated day, I stopped and asked myself, Why? Why was he so disruptive? In my darker moments I got caught up thinking that he was exhibiting these behaviors just to drive me crazy. He didn't like me. We were oil and water. He's just one of those kids.

Let me jump in and tell you that this isn't one of those stories where I end up being best friends with the student; he was challenging until the very last day of school. But when I started to think about why, it got a lot more sustainable. Special education teachers will often talk about antecedents—the events that set the behaviors in motion. Antecedents can explain a lot. It's relevant and important for all teachers to understand this.

So, back to my student: I was so busy responding to his behavior and playing whack-a-mole that I forgot to ask why he was exhibiting these behaviors. It was an all too familiar story: my student was a few grade levels behind and had serious work-avoidance issues. When it was time to sit down and actually get around to the math work his nervous system was on edge. He didn't want the other kids to see how behind he was, so he didn't want to work in partners or groups. But he didn't really know where to start on his own, so working alone wasn't an option either. His behavior was so disruptive that it was even difficult for me to put him in the small, teacher table group because then we wouldn't get much done.

His behavior was actually him communicating with me as best as he could. He was telling me that my time blocks were too long, that he felt left behind, and that I hadn't created access points into the material to meet him where he was at. As a 6th grader with limited communication skills, seeing a page full of word problems can be daunting. So he acted out. The more he acted out, the less he could tell what was going on, and the more he got behind—so the more he acted out. We were in a toxic cycle.

When I took myself and my feelings out of it, I could see the behavior for what it was—feedback—and make appropriate adjustments. Sometimes that meant chunking what he was working on so it was more approachable. Sometimes that meant timing myself so I could be mindful about how much time I spent talking. It wasn't always smooth, but we made progress.

When behaviors happen, especially big behaviors that disrupt your entire schedule, it's important to see behavior as feedback, and ask yourself, Why is my student behaving this way? Figure 3.1 shows what might be going through a student's head when they're acting out.

Figure 3.1 Consider the Student's Why

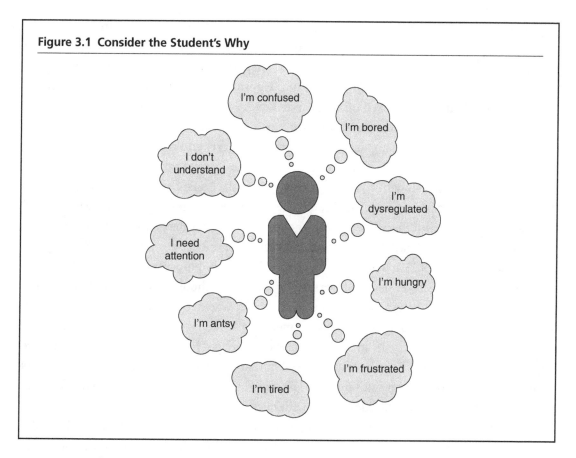

Mindset Shift 4: There's No Magic Wand

I love to tell stories about my students. I love to share about their triumphs, the happy moments that make teaching worth it. My favorites are the stories about kids who make a comeback. Those kids who struggled but then made amazing progress. Those stories can even inspire the kids who struggle to become teachers themselves.

Take a moment to reflect on your best turnaround story. Maybe it was a kid who came in at the beginning of the year way below grade level but then left at the top of the class. Maybe it's a student who was shy on day one but eventually opened up to become the class socialite. Maybe it was a student who had challenge after challenge all through December, but by March they were one of your best. Those heartwarming stories are important and will get you through some tough times.

But of course not all stories work out with a happy ending. I have my fair share of those stories, especially when I worked in middle school. I had students whom I pulled out all the stops for and poured my heart into. One student in particular, Martin, I still think about at least once a week. I wanted to see this kid *win*—we all did. He was a 7th grader who had had so many tough breaks at home. He checked off pretty much every adverse childhood experience in the book: challenges with substance abuse, domestic violence, and housing insecurity at home—not to mention the compounding impacts of concentrated poverty and racism.

At the time I was at a high-resource school and we really felt that we had the resources to support our challenging students. We tried every trick in the book: counseling, partnering with the family, positive reinforcement, breaks, flexible schedules, mentorship—to name a few. And there were good days with this student—even good weeks. But for the majority of the year it was pretty rough. There were days when I cried, days when he cried, days when I second-guessed everything about this job. We would have these breakthrough moments of clarity, and then the next day it was as if we never had a conversation. The entire school was committed to avoiding punitive measures such as suspension and expulsion unless someone's safety was in danger, but unfortunately there were some behaviors that meant this student had to do in-school suspensions a few times. Ultimately, I can't say that it ever really got better with Martin. There were bright spots and some really amazing moments, but that student had a difficult time in my class from the beginning of the year until the very last day. He had a difficult time the following year, and every subsequent year I stayed in touch with him.

When I first started researching and trying to learn more about anti-racism and asset pedagogies, I scoured books looking for answers about what to do with Martin. Was there a framework I should have employed? An approach I should have tried? Maybe he would have responded to a different extrinsic motivator? The reality is, I'm sure there were other practices that would have served him better, but nothing would be a magic wand that would change my student overnight.

The material reality is that kids develop at different times. As a teacher it can be frustrating to balance pushing kids forward and yet also understanding that they all have their own pace. There's so much development that can happen over the course of a single year: for example, kindergarteners can go from not being able to spell their names to reading short stories.

But behavior doesn't have the same ebb and flow as other types of learning. Behavior tends to come in crescendos and waves. At the beginning of the year, you'll spend quite a bit of time focusing on procedures and expectations. It might take some time for things to germinate and click for students—and then there'll be ups and downs throughout the year. One day you might feel like you found the magic wand—and then the next day you'll feel like it's the first day all over again.

I always strive to be realistic with the teachers I'm working with. You might have a year where your kids test you every single day. You can be highly effective and use all your tricks and still not see significant progress. This doesn't mean that you shouldn't still try to find practices that help your kids soar. But keep in mind, some classes are just tough. Sometimes I tell teachers, "The only way out is through."

You also might have students who never click with the classroom ecosystem but end up being highly successful later on in their academic careers. When I taught 6th grade I thought about my classroom as ground zero. I was preparing them for middle school, and the transition was sharp—from self-contained classes to having multiple teachers. In the end, I had many students who didn't click with school until 8th grade. Some 11-year-olds I experienced were completely different from the 14-year-olds my colleagues taught. Many of my middle-school students have checked in with me as high-school students and proudly declared they don't have any challenges with behavior—at least, not any more.

Regardless of any kid's individual progress, every student can experience joy in the classroom. They can feel cared for, and like they belong. Strive to create classroom ecosystems rooted in joy, belonging, and care—but remember that there won't always be a magic wand.

Mindset Shift 5: Understanding the Natural Ebbs and Flows of the Year

After teaching for a few years we get a feel for the natural ebb and flow of the school year. Every teacher has days when they feel they're truly and deeply living their purpose and days when they feel like they might not make it until the end of the year. The trick is to learn how to ride the natural ups and downs of the teaching experience.

Students take dramatic developmental leaps during the school year. As they get older they get more accustomed to the systems in the classrooms—and they just get better at being in school. This is why it's critical to see the overall arc of the year and not get too caught up in what might seem like slow progress.

You might notice spikes in behavior in October and March. In October, the luster of the beginning of the year has faded, but you aren't quite close to Thanksgiving break. In March, the year can drag unless you have an early spring break. Teachers can also be especially frustrated on the days right before breaks or on abnormal days. For me, it was always the time near Halloween, the day before December break, and the days before spring break. The kids felt it, and so did I. We all needed a break. In those moments I fantasized about running away and working at a coffee shop. There were days that I felt absolutely hopeless and questioned if I was really made for this.

If you have those days when you feel something similar, before you tender your resignation, think about the scope and flow of the year. Are breaks coming? Did the kids recently have a high-energy day like a festival or a field trip? Those feelings are completely valid, but it can help to know that you aren't alone, that it's expected to have great days and terrible days. You can also consider planning ahead. You can build in some self-care days ahead of time if you know that things are going to be a little bit bumpy!

Mindset Shift 6: Being in Community Is a Skill

School isn't just about learning academic skills. Our classrooms provide invaluable opportunities for students to learn collaborative life skills. Working together, communicating, taking turns are all part of learning how to be with others. In lower elementary especially, teachers invest significant time into building this toolbox for their students.

Some kids learn these skills at home. Playing with siblings and cousins is the first step for many students before they come to school and have to collaborate with dozens of strangers. But not all students come to school with this frame of reference, so it's critical that teachers understand that they are teaching life skills, especially with the youngest learners.

This was difficult enough before the pandemic, but the disruption of 2020 has made things more challenging. Now our students spend more and more time with technology and isolated from each other, so they are not building the early communication skills that we might expect.

Students are also learning to be in community with kids that are unlike them both culturally and racially. And though most children aren't being indoctrinated with racism at home—and they aren't born racist—children certainly see race. Children as young at nine months show preference for adults who look like them. Studies show that by kindergarten children consider race when picking playmates (Kinzler, 2016). For kids who live in homogenous communities, school could be their first opportunity to experience a heterogenous group. They come to the classroom with ideas from the media—and their parents—about race that the teacher has to help them unpack and navigate. And that's even before we consider other identity markers such as gender and class.

If we want safe, inclusive, and caring ecosystems, we have to be intentional about building them. It serves neither students nor teachers to assume that our students will automatically know how to be around each other. When you start to think about the classroom ecosystem, helping your students develop community-building skills will be critical.

CLASSROOM ECOSYSTEMS

Your classroom is a tiny ecosystem. The way that we approach keeping it healthy matters. Some of the mindsets we have been taught and experienced do not serve our classrooms well. We must move away from deficit mindsets about students and culture, and shift toward an asset-based approach, one where we recognize the role of joy. To build a healthy ecosystem, teachers must step into their own autonomy and sometimes shift their mindsets.

Mindset Shift 7: A Healthy School Culture Can Go Far

I worked at a K–8 early in my career called Loga Tuam that had an amazing school culture. It's become a north star for me when I talk about school culture. Here are some of the highly effective school-wide policies that made it easy to have healthy classroom cultures at that school:

The students were organized into families. These mixed-age groups met once a month and did a fun, usually seasonal activity together. Kids would stay in their family for their entire tenure at the school. They ended up building strong relationships with each other and their family's lead teacher. That person became another trusted adult who looked out for them.

Each year, each teacher picked one student who needed a little extra love. We divided up the students and became mentors for each other. The responsibilities were not overwhelming; our goal was simply to check up on these students and make them feel special and seen.

There was a thriving "Parent Squad." (I'm proud to say this was my contribution!) They met monthly and the principal sought their perspectives on all kinds of issues; they organized all the funraisers and fundraisers as well. All parents and family members were welcome to participate. The most consistent members were a fun group of moms whom I'm still in touch with to this day.

We had a school-wide SEL program. All teachers implemented the program, from kindergarten through 8th grade.

These policies produced an amazing school culture. Among ourselves, though teachers definitely ranted, there was a level of respect for students and families that was apparent in every conversation.

Teachers had fun with the kids. We would play with them at recess, chat with them in the mornings, and just had a general sense of closeness. It was cool to be a leader at this school, so we didn't have to deal with social script that getting in trouble was cool or exciting. Because of the heavy-handed culture building from kindergarten onward, the *kids* were invested in maintaining a healthy community.

All combined, having this strong school culture made it much easier for individual teachers to build strong classroom cultures.

Mindset Shift 8: You Set the Tone in the Classroom

I know that many schools don't quite have the same culture as Loga Tuam. The most common concern and question that I get from teachers is that they want to implement changes but their overall school-wide culture is toxic or dysfunctional. This is a very valid concern, but it's not impossible to overcome.

The first step to building the classroom ecosystem is recognizing the agency that you have over the classroom environment.

When I was at Loga Tuam, my classroom ecosystem thrived with a fairly simple system. First, I set my classroom up for success. I had a truly diverse set of kids that year: Vietnamese students, Shoshone students, Polynesian students, Filipino students, El Salvadorean students, Honduran students, and Black students. They had all heard all kinds of messages about each other's races in the media and from their families but I was determined to cultivate a community where they all felt included. I started with the visuals, making sure that everyone could see themselves in someone on the walls.

I had some students that were designated as ESL—that's what we were calling English language learners at the time—and a few IEPs. I arranged my classroom so that I could differentiate easily and use proximity for my chatty kids. *Using proximity* basically means being strategic about where I stood in the room. Kids tend to pay closer attention to you if you're close to them.

We had a classroom incentive that we worked toward each week, and students earned points that they could cash in for a coupon from my coupon box. I had coupons for things like using the teacher chair, lunch with the teacher, and a surprisingly popular stinky feet coupon that meant that you could remove your shoes. In this ecosystem, the students weren't caught up in the extrinsic motivation because there were already so many other things in our ecosystem that built their intrinsic motivation. The system wasn't punitive because they only earned points, never lost them.

On most days it was enough to tell kids that they got three reminders. If they had to get that second reminder we had a check-in conversation to make a plan to get back on track. The few times that we did have major behaviors my principal was incredibly supportive.

When it was time for me to move on to the next school, I brought my strategies along with me. I figured I'd set up a classroom just like my old one; I even had the same coupons. But my approach didn't land well with this new set of kids. The three reminders in particular didn't work; my students were absolutely unfazed by my stern looks and enumeration.

I'd thought we'd have an effective classroom culture—the students were a bit more homogenous, and I had a few years more of experience. But what I didn't account for was the school culture.

This school had had four different principals in two years. Most of the teachers were new, and we'd had a string of poor-data years, which meant that every PD was all about academics, never about culture. If there was a school-wide culture vision or even a plan, I was unaware of it. It was a very, very challenging year.

There were many factors at play, but I know that part of the reason why my plan fell flat was because there wasn't a school culture that the students had as a frame of reference. It was "every kid for themselves."

So what does that mean for teachers who are at schools that just can't seem to build that strong culture? You'll have to be even more mindful and intentional about building your own smaller ecosystem.

If your overall school culture is toxic and behaviors are trending toward negative and disruptive, it can be tempting to jump in and start thinking about consequences. Usually, the first question that teachers ask me is how to respond to a behavior: "What would you do if . . ." And although the more urgent concern might seem to be the negative behaviors, you might want to start with the proactive measures.

I ask teachers to first look around their classrooms and think through what they've already established:

- Does your room feel safe?
- Does it feel warm and welcoming?
- Do you think kids feel included when they walk in?
- Are there moments of joy?
- If they start feeling escalated or anxious, do they know what they can do?
- How do you celebrate wins with them?
- The behaviors certainly need a response, but to use a sports analogy: you have to think of offense, not just defense.

When I switched to the school with the not-so-great school culture, I went right into defense mode. I started getting more creative and doubling down on the punishments because that's what the other teachers were focused on. I almost forgot about all the wonderful, positive, and proactive things I had done at my Loga Tuam that had worked out so well. Sometimes the joy, the proactive measures, must come first.

In the absence of a clear mission and vision, kids will often create a culture that mimics what they see elsewhere. So start with the classroom ecosystem. Sometimes just one healthy classroom ecosystem can be the catalyst for school-wide change.

Mindset Shift 9: Proactive over Reactive

Much of management is framed as responding to student needs, but the most highly effective management is actually proactive. It's about creating the container for students to thrive in. It's about building a healthy ecosystem where students feel safe and like they belong.

I was chatting with a frustrated teacher from Michigan named Ms. Austin. She was recounting some of the challenging behaviors that she was experiencing in her classroom and asking for my advice. Students were rude to each other during group work, moved her personal items around, and talked over each other. Ms. Austin spent more than half of her day just trying to keep up with all the behaviors. She was there with another teacher Ms. Rodney in her grade level who was shocked to hear about the behavior. When Ms. Austin asked how Ms. Rodney did it, she responded that they would never even *think* of that kind of behavior in my classroom—it's just out of the question!

That is what we are going for. We aren't just thinking about stopping students from exhibiting these behaviors, we are talking about a classroom community that is so healthy, students don't think about these behaviors because they have respect for each other and the space. Planting seeds of empathy, respect, care, and community is *much* more effective than playing whack-a-mole with behavior after behavior.

I've worked with teachers at their wit's end, incredibly frustrated. They are perplexed and shocked by student behavior, exasperatedly shouting, "Why would they do this!?"

Sometimes my response is, "Well, why wouldn't they?"

It might sound strange but the reality is, kids are still learning about community and boundaries. If they are not in an environment where they feel safe and they are invested in the community, disruptive or harmful behaviors are not out of the question.

Take a minute to reflect on the classroom. Is it a space where these unsafe or inappropriate behaviors would be acceptable or shocking?

To help the classroom ecosystem start to take shape, begin with the proactive systems that will help your students invest in keeping it healthy.

Mindset Shift 10: Kids Don't Need to *Earn* Joy

Before the pandemic, a general best practice in trauma-informed care was that, for every one negative interaction with an adult, a student needed six positive interactions to make up for it.

If you're a teacher, take a moment and think through your last few days in the classroom: did you hit this ratio?

Having fun, smiling, enjoying yourself, and being excited to be at school are rights, not privileges. Students should never feel like they have to earn joy. Joy should be a baseline in the classroom and should be something that students can depend on, even if they're having a rough day. Too often I see schools taking away recess or not allowing certain students to participate in celebrations because of their behavior. Some teachers see it as an opportunity to reward a student, if they typically have challenging behaviors, maybe dangling an afternoon celebration will incentivize them to get on track. I understand where this might seem tempting, but we have to move away from taking away baseline experiences from kids because they struggle to make good choices. This can also have the opposite effect; students can become entrenched in a feedback loop, where they don't experience the positive aspects of school and grow to resent school and their teacher even more.

Think back to some of your most pivotal memories of school. Maybe it's a moment in class where you learned something, but right along with what you learned is probably a field trip or maybe a classroom celebration.

When I first started teaching I thought that these classroom celebrations were a great incentive to dangle in front of students to get them to "behave." Most of my 5th graders were pretty solid (one of the reasons why I'm still convinced 5th grade is one of the best ones to teach!) but I did have struggles with Celia. Celia was not responsive to my other behavior tactics like points and calling home, but she did love the holiday season and was incredibly excited for our "Winter Wonderland" party that was happening the day before winter break. Threatening her worked. For the weeks leading up, it was like teaching a different child. She wasn't perfect, but each time she seemed to be struggling I would give her a meaningful look and pointed to the countdown for the party and she would get back on track. It was going well.

Three days before the party, disaster struck. I'm not sure what else was going on with her but she was having a particularly rough day. She was escalated from morning line-up all the way until recess. She ended up pushing another student out of the way, taking the handball ball, and speaking disrespectfully to a rec aide. By my own metrics that I'd set in advance, she'd lost the right to attend the party. When the day came, Celia spent the afternoon of the party in the office with our office administrator. The other teachers and my school leader all thought that I did the right thing.

If I could go back, I would have done things differently. Here's why:

- The administrator had to miss all the fun, too.

- It might not have been developmentally appropriate to set a metric requiring that a student with a history of behavior challenges would have perfect behavior for six weeks straight.
- Celia missed out on the party and pictures and fun that the students had. Two years later, the other kids from her class were *still* talking about that party.
- Keeping her out made her feel even more isolated in the classroom community than she had before.
- Our community wasn't complete without her! The party was a fun culture builder, but it wasn't the same because not everyone was there.
- Celia didn't "learn her lesson"; she was just sad.

Reflecting on the incident, I can see that I was too focused on sticking to my guns. In the back of my mind was the cumulative impact that all of her behaviors had had on the classroom over the course of the year. I lost sight of what was best for my student.

Every situation is different, but as a general practice, I no longer use community builders and moments of joy to teach kids lessons. Feeling successful, joyful, and part of the group is exactly what struggling students need to get back on track!

Mindshift 11: Asset Versus Deficit Approach

Here's what the Association of College & Research Libraries (ACLU, 2020) has to say about asset-based teaching:

> Asset-based teaching seeks to unlock students' potential by focusing on their talents. Also known as strengths-based teaching, this approach contrasts with the more common deficit-based style of teaching which highlights students' inadequacies.

Basically, when you apply an asset approach, you see difference as an opportunity and diversity as an asset—not something to overcome. Consider this (re)framing: when talking about students of color, we often problematize their race and culture. We think of kids overcoming obstacles like neurodivergence, or not speaking English at home. If we approach students with a deficit mindset, then their cultural frames of reference become something that the teacher and student have to mitigate. But what if the student isn't the problem or the obstacle? What if we instead discussed how what we need to overcome is racism and systemic oppression, not a student's individual problem? A framing that focuses on leveraging what your students bring to the classroom sets up both teacher and student for success.

Here's an example of how an asset approach can make teaching more enjoyable and sustainable.

Dance trends come and go in pop culture. By the time you're reading this there'll probably be some new dance on TikTok (or maybe a future platform!) that the kids are all trying to learn.

When I first started coaching, the song "Hit the Quan" was all the rage. If this doesn't sound familiar it was a TikTok style dance craze before there really was a TikTok. The students loved that dance—all it took was one student to start singing and they all joined in. When I first noticed it, I was too entertained to see it as a behavior problem. These were amazingly well-coordinated 2nd graders! They had more rhythm than some adults! They hyped each other up and were so joyful. I tried (and failed) to learn it after spending an embarrassing amount of time studying the moves at recess.

Later that day I was observing Norah, a teacher on my coaching load. Even when I wasn't officially coaching teachers on anti-racist practices—because the term *anti-racist* wasn't in the common lexicon—I was still thinking about helping my teachers be more culturally responsive. The teachers whom I worked with were all white, and all the students were Black and Brown.

I stepped into Norah's classroom, took a seat, and watched quietly for about 45 minutes. In our debrief when I talked to Norah about the time I'd spent observing, I was ready to talk about some pedagogical moves that she could make that would be more aligned with culturally responsive practices. But she wanted to talk about behavior. Almost through tears, she apologized profusely and said that she was embarrassed by her students' behavior; she told me that they acted like "that" even when the principal was in the room observing. The "that" was the dancing. In between transitions, from seats to rug or to line-up, more than once a student would call out "Hit the Quan!" and at least a handful would do the dance. These were not the "calm bodies" that Norah had asked for during the transition. To the kids' credit, the dance was not disruptive. They did their little moves, laughed, and ultimately ended up where they needed to be in a reasonable amount of time.

Norah and I clearly saw the dancing very differently. I saw the energy and joy as an asset. I've personally experienced how difficult it can be to get joy going in a classroom when students are just too downtrodden to be joyful. I assured her that some teachers would greatly appreciate having kids who were so energetic! The consequences of having a school culture rooted in control is that when it's time for students to be joyful or excited, they don't see school or the classroom as a place where that can happen!

When I saw Norah's kids I thought of all the ways that we could channel that energy and use it to bolster the overall sense of community in the classroom. "I just can't get them to stop dancing!" she said emphatically. My response was simple: "Why do they have to stop dancing?"

Obviously the classroom can't be a 24/7 dance party (as much as I'd like it to be). There is work to be done. Learning needs to happen, and dance breaks are not always safe. But I saw their energy as a solution, not a problem. We could use that energy. I pushed Norah to reframe how she was thinking about school and classrooms. Why can't "Hit the Quan" be part of our routine?

We decided to change our approach. When we did, Norah was less frustrated, and the kids were just as joyful and they were even more productive. We decided to have designated dance breaks, and the kids would work to earn some extra time at the end of the day to teach Norah the dance. The students even had a dance-off with the winner getting access to her treasure box. This gave students in her class who didn't always experience success academically the chance to feel like something they brought to the table was of value.

When you have an asset-based approach, recognize that you are actively pushing back against systems of oppression. Our school system was designed to see any student who doesn't conform as a deficit. But when you flip this around, and see the students in the fullness of their humanity as assets, you resist oppression and help liberate their potential and make space for joy. And this doesn't just apply to teaching—it applies to all aspects of life.

Mindset Shift 12: Quiet and Compliant Doesn't Always Mean Productive

I've had the pleasure of working with students K–12. The longer you spend around all the ages, the more you'll see the difference between the younger and older students. Kindergarteners are joyful and enthusiastic about school. It is very rare to see young students who don't like school. They love their teachers and they're excited to come each day. Slowly but surely things start to change. Those bright-eyed babies grow up and begin to resent school. To a certain extent this is usual—kids are exposed to more, have hormonal changes, and mature—but some of the shift is related to the cumulative wearing down of their spirits, joy, and enthusiasm.

When I worked with kindergarteners, I had a student named Ronni. She was a ray of sunshine. Her behavior was frequently disruptive and she was rarely where she was supposed to be, but she was just so *fun*. I thought of her as joy personified. And she *loved* school—she literally skipped into the classroom each day with her hair beads clacking. But schools weren't meant to foster the joy in students like Ronni. She was frequently disciplined because she would rather dance than sit still, and her naturally booming voice wasn't always suitable for quiet work time.

Years later, I saw her at the movies with a group of her friends; she was in middle school at the time. I was so excited to hear about how she had progressed and all the wonderful things that she was doing. When I talked to her, she told me about how her teachers didn't understand her and she was often in trouble. She said, "You know me, Ms. Smith, I hate school."

I was absolutely shocked. The little girl I knew was loved by all and had adored school! How did this ray of sunshine, a student who couldn't wait to get into the building, turn into a kid whose hatred of school became a core part of her identity?

Her biggest challenge was that she just was not quiet. She was not the student who jumped into to quiet study time right away. She did not do what her teachers asked her right away. She would rather skip, sing, or dance than walk quietly with hands at her side.

But why is it so important that our classrooms are quiet? Kids need to be able to focus and concentrate on their work, but any teacher will tell you that kids can be just as off-task quietly as they can be loudly. The idea that the classroom has to have a hushed tone is even on some rubrics for teacher evaluation! The idea that quiet always means learning is not aligned with culturally relevant or responsive best practices. Some cultures are more collaborative in their learning structure, meaning that the quiet siloed learning experience isn't conducive to their learning— and, predictably, those kids give you feedback in the form of disruptive behavior.

Eventually, kids get worn down. Rules and expectations that exist only to control them, and systems rooted in white supremacy culture that don't leave space for their individual expression take their toll. Eventually, a high-spirited, loving child can be transformed. Noisy, high-energy classes can still be productive and allow your students to thrive.

Mindset Shift 13: IEPs Don't Mean Lower Expectations

I was visiting a school in San Diego and a teacher, Grace, asked to come and take some notes on her behavior response. The idea was that after the observations I would give her some things to think about and some strategies to improve the classroom culture. I observed her for an entire day, and I sat in the back and took notes, watching some very strong practices that she used in the classroom but I also noticed a few things that she could tweak to get even better.

We sat down and talked over coffee. I jumped into my notes, I started to talk about a particular student named Liam and ask her some questions about her approach. I noticed that Liam was a classic attention seeker. He would chatter over her and do silly things like poke other students. When he got desperate he'd walk around, make noises, and do everything he could to get a rise out of the other kids. His teacher studiously ignored him. I typically recommend this practice for handling that type of behavior. It can be effective to ignore the negative behaviors, then reward the student with attention when they are participating appropriately. But even when Liam would get back on track, Grace left him to his own devices for the most part. I didn't notice her interacting with him for the entire day.

I brought him up, and Grace dismissed me. "Oh he's one of my IEPs so don't worry about him. I don't need your advice on him." Respectfully, I felt like she did need my advice! Liam was treated like a pariah in the classroom and the students were following her lead.

When I pressed she told me that she used to have regular meetings with the inclusion teacher, but they had petered off. The caseloads were just too overwhelming and they had more severe challenges to tackle. They had recently had an annual meeting so Grace wasn't planning on checking in with the family for a while. Her plan was to continue as normal and ignore him for the most part.

It is critical that teachers understand when we say a classroom community, we mean *all* the students. Not all the gen-ed students, not all the well-behaved students—all of them.

For Grace, the fact that Liam had an IEP meant that he somehow didn't count and that she didn't need to actively engage him in the community. With few exceptions, if a student is in a classroom with other students without IEPs, you can assume that they have the capacity to participate in the classroom community meaningfully. The goal of IEPs is for students to be able to participate in learning environments *with* their peers.

There are many equity issues for students with IEPs but to start, whatever their eligibility is, they are legally and ethically entitled to the same classroom experiences as other students. The IEP itself should help the general education teacher, SPED teacher, and the family establish a plan and a road map for the student to be successful in the classroom. But it doesn't work if the document becomes an excuse to lower expectations and hold the student back from being a part of the classroom ecosystem. They should feel like they belong and are cared for as well.

In my experience teachers and families can get frustrated and confused by the IEP process. It can create a point of contention, and it can have serious implications for the student's future. If a student qualifies for services, then they are entitled to them. But the solutions and services granted in the IEP should work in tandem with the existing plan in the classroom. If you have a student whom you think might qualify for an IEP, but you find yourself in the long waiting process, you can anticipate what strategies and methods might be recommended in the IEP and just start implementing them. When that student does start to receive services, that means that the gen-ed teacher works in tandem with other service providers and is still very much a critical part of the students' education.

Early in my career I had a very challenging student in the 5th grade. Many people around me told me that it would be much easier if her family would let her get some services. Hailey's family did not want to engage in any kind of process because they did not want their child to be labeled, and although it was initially frustrating, I completely understood. According to the National Center for Learning Disabilities, Black students are overrepresented in SPED and disproportionally restrained. Latinx students are also overrepresented, especially in speech and language services (NCLD, 2020). I was really struggling with her and her behavior. I leaned on the veteran teachers in my school and went to a few extra PDs on the curriculum so I could figure out how to give her access points to what we were learning, but her behavior was still very difficult for me to handle. I had no idea for sure, but I thought she might have some kind of ADHD and so did her family.

After I got tired of trying to push the family to get her support, my principal gave me some advice that I still live by today. You don't need to wait for a test to find strategies that work for your students.

So I went to Google. I looked up "Strategies for ADHD students" and to my surprise there were plenty of suggestions that were easy to implement and that I could start right away! I started implementing these practices in my classroom in general and found that they worked well for all of my students!

I tried three things: three breaks per day when she could take a lap and run around the track one time, a seat closer to me with a rubber band around the desk that she could play with her feet (a Pinterest find!), and check-ins with me once a week. I shared all this with her family at a meeting, and I told them we'd have a follow-up meeting in two months. I will never know what an IEP might have said, but my little plan was highly effective! She wasn't perfect, but with these things in place we were actually able to enjoy each other instead of me constantly responding to her behaviors.

Maybe the IEP process would have been more beneficial, or maybe she didn't even have ADHD, but I had to let go of the mindset that either of those things would have changed the fact that, ultimately, it was my responsibility to find a way for her to thrive in our classroom community.

IEPs are a valuable resource for both students and teachers. They should be used to help the student thrive in the classroom community—not divest from it.

BEYOND MANAGEMENT AND PUNISHMENT

One of the most fundamental roles of a teacher is to keep students safe. For kids to be joyful and feel like they belong, there needs to be some level of organization, structure, and safety. There is a fine line to walk between making space for joy and ensuring that students are safe and responsible. But unfortunately some teachers spend too much time thinking about controlling what goes on in their classroom, and not enough time thinking about building a strong classroom community.

Title 1: Shorthand for "Most Difficult"

There is a persistent perception in teaching that Title 1, or urban, or inner-city schools are more challenging because the students are further "behind" or that the behaviors are worse. When teachers want to convey that their jobs are challenging, some even use *Title 1* as shorthand for "most difficult." This has not been my experience. It's true that Title 1 schools have unique challenges, but I don't believe that students can be "behind" when the metric they're being judged by is high-stakes standardized tests and standards that have been proven to be ineffective and racist. All schools have behavior challenges—they're just different challenges.

Mindset Shift 14: Safe Communities, Not Controlled Classrooms

When teachers talk about expectations or rules I ask them, is this about control and compliance? Or community and safety?

Consider the following rules or expectations:

- Sitting a particular way in a chair
- Having bathroom passes
- (Always) standing in a straight line
- Silent work time

Now any classroom teacher knows that there are plenty of reasons why these rules would sometimes be necessary for safety or productivity reasons, but having these as expectations or rules *always* is more about control than safety.

When you focus on a safe community, and not just a well-controlled community, students are able to be joyful and the fullest version of themselves. When students do something that is harmful or breaks down the community in some way, the response should not just be to demand compliance. Compliance for the sake of compliance doesn't necessarily help kids learn and grow. Instead, your response should help students understand that there are expectations for how they interact with their teachers and classmates to keep them safe.

I once worked with a 1st-grade teacher, Ms. Haley, who had been teaching for a decade but had the most chaotic classroom I have ever seen. She had the classic checkered-square rug, but she was not particular about how students sat in their squares. She had no line order. No behavior management systems—no marbles, clips, nothing. And yet she had the highest scores, the happiest kids, and the fewest referrals to the office. Families would literally bribe the office coordinator to be on her roster. And she had the same population as all the other teachers—all BIPOC, low-income, and mostly emergent bilingual kids. She had one of the strongest communities I had ever seen. Her students were truly joyful and worked together beautifully. She built a healthy ecosystem and let it thrive. I wish I could bottle some of her magic. What made her different? She was all about creating the community. For the first two months of school things were a bit rough. There were a lot of songs, time for practice, and "redos." Regardless of what was happening in the classroom, the kids were always at the center. They talked to each other about challenges, they reflected together when the community got off track, they were invested in creating and maintaining a healthy classroom community. She was consistent and patient and, by November, it had paid off.

I never heard her talk about compliance. I only heard her helping kids understand consequences, community, and safety. She showed us that a healthy ecosystem could exist without a focus on compliance and control.

What Makes Good Management

When I was a student I was always in a classroom with very few behavior issues. I always thought I'd be the kind of teacher with "good management" when I entered the field. My personal experience was reinforced by my mentors. I listened to the mentors who encouraged me to run a tight ship with my Black and Brown students in Oakland, California. A teacher who was held in very high regard and had even won international teaching awards told me about his effective classroom management strategy. He said it was simple: you just had to have high expectations for effort, behavior, and respect. Like a good pupil I put those words up on the wall and waited to see what would happen.

Our process was straightforward: you either earned or lost points on Class Dojo for effort, behavior, and respect—and at the end of the week you went home with a report for your parents to sign. Simple, and by many metrics, it actually worked very well.

My students were known school-wide for their good behavior. We were complimented at assemblies and other teachers would send their kids to my class for a few minutes when they needed a stern talking to. "I'm going to send you to Ms. Smith!" became a thing. I didn't mind. I was proud of my classroom and it felt good to have order when so many of my colleagues were struggling. When I told people that I taught in Oakland they automatically assumed that my students would have many behavior issues. I always told them that they never gave me any problems and waited for the impressed look to cross their face.

(continued)

When I reflect on that time, I'm not as proud. At the end of the year, I was rated highly effective on my evaluations, but was I?

If effective meant that my kids did what they were told, how I told them to do it, then yes, I was.

But were they joyful?
Did they feel like the fullest and best versions of themselves?
Did I teach them to take pride in their culture or themselves?
Did I make them feel seen?
Did they learn to be in community?
Did they know I cared about them?
Did they feel like they belonged?
Maybe, but it wasn't because of anything that I did intentionally.

I had to reframe what success in the classroom looked like for myself. That started with the internal work. Black and Brown folks have to unlearn systems of oppression just like white folks. As a Black woman, I had to recognize that I was perpetuating the very system that made my own life so difficult. I struggled to meet the expectations of my teachers because they were not culturally responsive. I had to learn to perform every day. Why then, when I became the teacher, did I try and force the same system on my students? To begin to undo this for myself, and ultimately my students, I had to rethink what high performing really means.

When I think now about my classroom ecosystem, the first thing I ask myself is not about compliance. I don't measure effectiveness by my kids doing exactly what I want them to do, how and when I want them to do it. But for too many of us, that has become the marker of success. Do my kids sit silently and follow directions perfectly cannot be the only test.

It's time to redefine what good management really looks like.

Expectations that focus on control limit what students can do; expectations that focus on how to be in community with each other liberate what students can do.

Mindset Shift 15: Classrooms Should Be Managed

One of the fundamentals of teaching is behavior or classroom management. It's a phrase that almost everyone in the world of education uses to describe what goes on in classrooms apart from academics. Typically, you have one teacher, maybe two, and up to 35 students. How does one adult keep up to 35 children safe and ensure they learn the standards? Behavior management or classroom management. But what does management really mean?

According to the *Oxford Dictionary*,

Management (*noun*): The process of dealing with or controlling other people.

Do we want to control our students?

Think of your ideal classroom. Do you see yourself controlling students? Would you be dealing with them? Or would you be keeping them safe, engaging, and interacting?

The words that we use to describe our classroom matters.

If we frame what we do as management, then the teacher, the manager, takes a central role. The teacher is ultimately at the top of the hierarchy because they are the manager. If you've ever worked outside of the field of education, you might have had someone whose formal title was *manager* working over you. That person was probably checking your clock-in times, approving your PTO, and making sure you followed company policies.

There are some managerial aspects to running a classroom. It is ultimately the teacher's responsibility to make sure everyone is learning. It makes sense that a teacher guides and leads the classroom culture. But that doesn't mean that the classroom needs a hierarchy. If we remove the teacher for the top of the hierarchy, and instead place them in community with the students, it becomes the role of the entire community to keep things in balance.

Think of the classroom as an ecosystem, a web of interconnected relationships. Although the teacher is the leader and the responsible adult, it's not only on them to keep the classroom ecosystem functioning. That is why it's so critical for students to be active partners in shaping the community. They are responsible for keeping it healthy and thriving alongside the teacher.

To call this *management* puts the teacher in a procedural role that doesn't leave room for community or relationships. It disempowers the students and limits the agency they have within the classroom.

When teachers focus too much on being managers, they end up focused on policing behavior. When we police behavior our focus is on compliance, making sure all the students are following the expectations and rules. We do this hoping to keep kids safe, but this approach isn't always efficient or effective. How much time do teachers spend playing whack-a-mole and circling their classroom from table to table? What could we do with the energy that we aren't spending policing student's every move?

Sometimes we get so stuck on managing and policing, we forget to even step back and ask why the rules and policies exist, or why students might have a hard time following them.

The day I first became a dean, I became the school cop. We were fortunate not to have police on campus, but my function was the same. I went from classroom to classroom putting out fires and talking students down. My walkie-talkie went off all day. Maybe 7th grade was having a good day, but 6th grade had a sub, and we all knew what that meant. Maybe one of my "high-needs" students was absent, but it rained so the kids had indoor recess so the last half of the day was chaos. I knew several caregivers' cell and work phone numbers by heart. I was exhausted. The teachers were so past burn out, they had all but given up.

One week I decided to look at the data on the behavior referrals that came to my office. Most of them were for infractions such as talking in the hall, not wearing the correct uniform, or arriving to class tardy. Though these behaviors were disruptive, they weren't causing significant harm to the classroom communities. The behaviors were frustrating, and technically they weren't appropriate. Early in my career, I had been advised to push for 100% compliance with rules and expectations because it's a "slippery slope": once students start breaking one rule, they'll break them all. I was sharing my frustrations with a good friend of mine who's an ER nurse and she told me about triage and how it made things more manageable at the hospital. She explained that when everything is going wrong, you have to take a step back and figure out which challenges require the most urgency. You simply can't do it all. Not everything can be dealt with at once. She encouraged me to try and apply that same logic to my classroom.

As a "manager", I wanted to enforce all the rules. They were norms that I had inherited and they existed for a reason, but I spent a disproportional amount of energy on what I would call low-stakes issues. In hindsight there were certainly rules that were rooted in white supremacy culture that should have been changed anyway. But in the moment it was obvious that my mind-set as a manager wasn't allowing me to appropriately triage. For every conversation I had with a student about a crop top, I could have been building relationships with a kid who was struggling or stepping in to a classroom so a teacher could have a break.

Management will have you caught up in the weeds of policing behaviors, never stepping back to look at the full landscape. Teachers are not always in the position to actually change rules, and students absolutely must understand accountability. However, when you step away from a manager mindset, you can be more strategic. I started to ask myself different questions. What was I doing to build the community outside of policing its members? How could I be more efficient with my time?

Moving away from management benefits teachers and students. The mental stress and weight of managing 30+ people is heavy. When teachers start to see behavior for what it is—feedback— they free themselves from the stress of singlehandedly managing their classrooms.

Monitoring Versus Policing

When we center control, we can find ourselves policing. There are plenty of apps and systems designed to help teachers monitor and police student behavior. It's not without reason. There are students who are monitored because they have an upcoming eligibility determination for additional support or services. You might be monitoring student behavior to communicate progress with a family or share some positives and good news. There are good reasons to document and pay attention to what students are doing in the classroom, but it's critical to not slip into policing. Policing is what happens when we dehumanize students. We give them a label, we decontextualize their behavior, such as forgetting about underlying trauma and situational factors, and we are focused on controlling them to get a specific outcome instead of supporting them as a community member.

Mindset Shift 16: "Good" Schools Keep Kids Under Control

What makes a good school? Typically, when someone is trying to validate the worthiness of a school, the first thing to consider is test scores. Even though we know that standardized tests do little to help students learn, use up significant instructional time, and are often rooted in racism, we still use test scores to talk about "good" and "bad" schools. Most of these "bad" schools just happen to be the ones with high populations of Black and Brown students. These "bad" schools struggle with recruitment and retention for both teachers and students. Some of these "bad" schools will become "turnaround" schools. It varies from state to state, but some districts reserve the right to take control over low-performing schools to get them back on track. Usually that includes some kind of zero-tolerance policy. To "turn around" a "bad" school, highly regimented, strict, and disciplined practices might be implemented as a way to "get kids under control."

To be honest when I first started teaching I subscribed to this mentality. I thought that a good classroom meant that the teacher was totally in control, that the kids sat quietly and showed intense self-control.

I was lucky enough to have a school leader who allowed us to go see other schools and other ways of running a classroom. Sometimes, you just need to see best practices in action. My grade-level team and I went on a few school visits with the mindset that the "good" schools I'd see would be ones where kids were "under control." We went to some of the "high-performing" charter schools on the East Coast. These massive charter organizations had strict rules and expectations and codes. They ran like little factories, churning out students that conformed to all the school's values and character pillars. These schools were the model when I first became a teacher because they were getting publicity, huge donations, and had year-long waiting lists. As I walked through the schools I saw a few similar patterns. The ones that did talk about joy had a very narrow window and perspective about what joy looked like. Some schools called it *zest* and it meant something like clapping along with the class at an assembly. When you walked through the classrooms the kids were incredibly well programed to talk to guests. They worked quietly and were well organized. The teachers had a clear control of their classroom and moved incredibly methodically. Students worked toward getting a certain number of points each week to attend a Friday Fiesta. If they didn't get enough points they wrote out reflection sheets with the dean. Along with their parents, they kept track of their points on an app that teachers were persistent about updating. It worked; the kids were visibly and vocally very concerned about their points. There were few interruptions throughout the day. By all measures, they were successful.

Most of the high-performing charter schools operated this way and were for the most part Black and Brown. The fact that their students weren't white was further proof for many of the people there that they were doing good work. They had BIPOC kids scoring almost as well as white kids—and for that fact alone they were given credibility.

On the last day of our school visits, we went to a slightly different school. This was a charter but in a very high-resourced and white part of the metro area. There were some similarities with the other schools we'd visited, but what was most important were the differences we noticed.

The kindergarten class was, dare I say, chaotic compared to the other school. I could see on the board that they had two recesses each day. The kids were engaged in what the teacher called *inquiry play*, which seemed to involve exploring manipulatives, sensory boards, and open-ended literacy games. It was loud. There were plenty of different types of seats and a sensory table. The teacher, who was incredibly patient, was hosting a small group of students who were practicing fine motor skills—while the other students buzzed from station to station.

When we went to the 3rd-grade class we saw their free-choice time, which happened for an hour every day. Most kids were cluttered around the Tinker Table, where they played with developmentally appropriate engineering toys. In the middle of the visit, two students began fighting over something at the Tinker Table. When the teacher noticed she started singing the community meeting song. Slowly but surely each student dropped what they were doing (albeit sadly) and made their way to the carpet. They reviewed the agreements for free choice together and did a little cheer before going back to their stations.

In middle school I had the pleasure of seeing the Genius Hour. A student explained to me that at Google they apparently have a Genius Hour where employees are able to pursue their ideas and innovations. Genius Hour was just that. Students could use either the Maker Space or their own technology to work on exploratory projects. They sat wherever they wanted, listened to music, and just kind of explored. One student was slowly and tediously looking for outdated Wikipedia pages and doing research to update them. Another student was working on an app that she hoped to one day design. (I won't share the app idea, just in case—but it was a good one!) When I spoke with their teacher she told me that, when challenges arise, they use peer mediators for most issues. A student who is a trained mediator helps the students in conflict come to some kind of resolution. If they can't solve it among themselves, it's escalated to an adult. The students begin mediator training in 1st grade.

If this sounds too good to be true, I felt the same way while I was there. It was so different from the tightly controlled schools we'd been visiting. These students were actually as collaborative and cooperative with each other as the kids at the other charter schools, but the energy was just so different. It didn't seem like teachers had a need to feel in control. There was a sense of kids being kids, of social and emotional freedom. The school put a lot of emphasis on innovation and inquiry. They talked over and over about being curious and exploring. That attitude helped the students cultivate a sense of freedom and safety. Predictably, this school had even better test scores than did the "high-performing" charter schools.

The environment and ecosystem I experienced was clearly cultivated through extensive preparation, research, and intention. The school experienced very little turnover of students or teachers, most of whom were veteran.

Whether or not I could go back to my school and implement everything I've seen, it was so impactful to just see that there was another way. My narrow view of a "high-performing" school had been expanded. Too many stakeholders in education think "high-performing" schools with Black and Brown students have to be highly regimented schools.

The "high-performing schools" that I've seen with a majority white population approach pedagogy differently. They seek a level of creativity, inquiry, and expression. Some teachers will note that when those structures aren't in place, classrooms and school cultures can become negative and unsafe. But other schools who don't so heavily emphasize compliance and control can still be safe and positive. Remember, we are not just trying to manage our classrooms, but rather build healthy ecosystems.

Just because it's a formidable challenge doesn't mean the classroom can't start to move away from control and closer to joy, belonging, and care.

Mindset Shift 17: Consequences over Punishments

Strong classroom cultures are not founded on punishments; they're founded on consequences. Punishments are all about making students feel bad or experience negative feedback as the result of their actions. Consequences are all about students understanding that certain behaviors will trigger a response that they must be held accountable for. Consequences are about learning. There is a world of difference in these two approaches.

Why are there so many punishments in schools? Because we're still growing away from the punishment mindset, and because punishing is quicker and easier. When teachers are overworked and overwhelmed, it's hard to find the energy or inspiration to repeatedly respond only constructively. This is often when we see teachers slip into punishment mode. It's common and very easy to react this way. We lose sight of the humanity of the student and just see their actions.

But not dishing out punishments to students doesn't mean that those students aren't held accountable for their actions. Accountability is critical in every system—particularly in anti-racist or culturally responsive approaches. Kids have to understand that their actions might not be making others feel like they belong and are safe. But accountability isn't as easy and clean cut as punishments. It takes more time and more brain power. Many schools, for example, that use restorative justice don't have clear or strong accountability measures so it can seem like "nothing happens." This is where the myth of "doing nothing" comes in (to follow).

When teachers say they want "something" done, they're usually talking about a punishment, not a consequence, because our sense of retribution kicks in. In these moments, it's important to refresh your memory with Mindset Shift1: Kids Aren't Little Adults. Students' brains are not yet wired to fully grasp the long-term implications of their actions.

Ask yourself, do I want my student to feel bad, or do I want them to acknowledge the harm that they might have caused? Do I want them to understand that there are logical consequences to their actions, both in school and in the real world? Or do I want them to miss out on something to ease my own sense of right and wrong?

If shifting your mindset away from punishment and toward consequence feels like a tall order, you're in good company. Keep at it.

Restorative Justice

For those unfamiliar with restorative justice, here's a Cliff Notes version.

Restorative justice is not just another classroom management tool. Restorative practices are an alternative to the conventional way we think about discipline. In restorative justice, the focus is to repair harm. The process involves both students and educators. Some of the goals in restorative practices are to:

➢ Bring the parties together in a dialogue
➢ Make space for both parties to understand the harm that was caused
➢ Look for a pathway to heal and repair the harm
➢ Find some common ground and an agreement to move forward

In restorative justice, we look beyond the concept of punishment to instead aim for enabling students with the agency to address harm and repair relationships.

Mindset Shift 18: The Myth of "Doing Nothing"

When I worked in Northern California, I worked with some really amazing veteran teachers. They were especially helpful at showing me the ins and outs of how to navigate the politics of being part of a large district that has its own distinct challenges. These veteran teachers were incredibly comforting and had so much wisdom to share. For many teachers, myself included, the learning you do on the job from other teachers around you is even more impactful than your credentialing program.

These women became teachers in a very different time than I did—and from their vantage point, the schooling in the United States had changed dramatically. Whether it was the reality or their perception, they experienced students as more disrespectful and families as less cooperative than in their early days. They saw the less-punitive measures that many districts were adopting like restorative justice and were concerned that, at the end of the day, this boiled down to "doing nothing." In my work I have spoken with hundreds of teachers who feel the same way. There is a very serious and widespread concern that our students are not held accountable for their actions. But doing "something" doesn't necessarily mean punishment.

Veteran and novice teachers alike have that one student. For a teacher I worked with in the Bay Area, Ms. Martinez, this student was Johnny. Johnny just got under her skin. He wasn't received by all the teachers that way, but for some reason Ms. Martinez and Johnny were just oil and water. Our school was fairly progressive, so all teachers were trained in humanizing practices such as trauma-informed care and restorative justice. We assumed the best of Johnny and saw him in all his complexity. He was a good kid in certain classes and eager to help some teachers—but then he all but shut down for other teachers. We didn't know too much about what was going on at home, but we knew it deeply affected him.

What was interesting was that Johnny's behaviors rarely involved other students; he was focused on disrupting Ms. Martinez. It started off with small things, like a laser pointer and interrupting her during direct instruction. Before long, his behavior escalated. Midyear, someone broke one of her coffee mugs. We didn't have hard evidence, but all signs pointed to Johnny. At this point, Ms. Martinez was highly agitated; she was understandably taking it personally that Johnny was targeting her in particular. Our principal was supportive, but we were still trying to use restorative and humanizing practices rather than punishment. Our principal offered to do an admin shadow; we talked to the parents; we held circles—all the "best practices" in the book. Ms. Martinez was getting more and more frustrated. To her, because the behaviors continued, it felt like our principal was doing "nothing." She said, "I'm basically being attacked and he's doing nothing! I'm basically the victim of a crime!"

The final straw came when Johnny stole something out of her desk. She threatened to quit. She was utterly defeated.

As much as we need to humanize the student, it's critical to recognize the humanity of teachers as well. She was dedicated to her job and loved being with the kids. She was incredibly hardworking and patient and had been at the school for 10 years. She'd seen all kinds of behaviors. As kids are working through their trauma and challenges, someone has to be there along with them, giving them grace. That's what Ms. Martinez had been doing for decades, but giving kids grace takes energy, and Ms. Martinez was tapped out.

Our principal was in a difficult position. He strove to see the humanity of the student and be restorative, but at the same time it was clear that the situation was not working. Ms. Martinez wanted the student expelled; when you're personally affected and harmed, it can be very difficult to let go of the desire for "justice," when it's actually usually just revenge. She had found the old handbooks and learned that, before we switched to restorative approaches, Johnny would have been gone six incidents earlier. She was also concerned about other students: she wanted to send a message. If other students perceived that there were no consequences to Johnny's behavior, then what would stop them from doing the same? But expulsion was out of the question for our school; there was a district-wide moratorium on expulsions. A student had to be a serious safety threat for the conversation to be even opened. But what would make sense for us to do?

Ultimately our principal decided to move Johnny from her roster, host a restorative circle, and assign Johnny "community service" hours after school. That was the last time Johnny exhibited such extreme behaviors, but Ms. Martinez was still deeply hurt by the situation.

I empathize with her. A lot of teachers have complained to me that administrators "do nothing." There is even a rumor, based in some truth, that when some kids are sent out of class they return with candy or a treat. This does happen, but the intention of the treat is not to reward the behavior—it's intended as a de-escalation tool. Although I've never given out candy, I did work in a school where a student, Emily, had tantrums in her kindergarten classroom. She'd tear things off the wall in full-scale melt-down mode; she had some big feelings that her six-year-old body just couldn't communicate well. When I finally got her out of the room and into my office, I was able to calm Emily down by letting her rifle through my expansive sticker box. That was the only thing that would calm her enough to have a conversation. Perhaps her teacher thought I was "doing nothing" or rewarding her, but by February we were down to one tantrum per month—whereas we'd started at one per week. The stickers were not the magic wand, but they certainly helped Emily start to trust me.

But, given that many teachers feel like administrators do "nothing," our frame of reference regarding what we see as a response—a "something"—needs to be broadened. A student coming back to class (with a treat) doesn't necessarily mean nothing has been done if they're calmed down; a student being regulated enough to go back to class is actually a victory! The goal is for the student to be learning, so once the student has learned how to calm down—and after both the teacher and student have had a break—ultimately, that student needs to be in class.

In a report on the impact of discipline on instruction, "Lost Instruction: The Disparate Impact of the School Discipline Gap in California," it is estimated that more than 840,000 days of instruction are lost cumulatively throughout California when students are out of their classrooms—in one school year alone. This disproportionately affects Black students, who lose on average 32 more days of instruction than their white counterparts (Losen & Whitaker, 2017). Is it any wonder that Black students are falling behind? They spend less time in class.

It's true that sometimes nothing is done at the exact moment that a student is acting out. The administrator may need to confer with a specialist, the SPED teacher, the family—or just need more time to map out a response that isn't only punitive. And because our knee-jerk reaction is often to jump to a punitive response, taking some time can be valuable to create a meaningful, well-thought-out consequence.

That being said, there are some administrators out there who are in over their heads and are indeed doing nothing. I have worked with school leaders who simply did not address behaviors that harmed teachers and students. Sometimes they were overwhelmed. Sometimes they didn't take teachers seriously, and other times they just didn't know what to do. But setting those outliers aside, it's still true that if we're going to build a healthy classroom ecosystem that is rooted in joy, belonging, and care, we must expand our imagination of what an effective behavior response could look like, how long it takes, and what it really means to give consequences over punishments.

Mindset Shift 19: The Myth That Restorative Justice "Doesn't Work"

This isn't a book dedicated to restorative justice, but when done right, restorative justice can be a powerful and transformative approach to classroom cultures. (For a quick primer, see the sidebar on restorative justice.) If your school is implementing restorative justice, or you'd like to learn more about it, I would highly recommend doing further research. When done right, restorative justice can be highly effective. Many schools have seen a reduction in suspensions and higher sense of community with students.

But that's not the experience of every teacher. Many have shared frustration that restorative practices don't lead to cohesive and productive classroom communities. Unfortunately, when many schools shift to restorative practice they focus only on removing harsh punishments (which is a good thing) and implementing community circles. Community circles are a wonderful tool to build relationships, but they can't exist only as a response to harmful behaviors. Many of the teachers whom I have worked with and have a negative view of restorative justice are actually just working at schools where it has not been implemented well.

I worked with a teacher in the Midwest whose school was dealing with some serious behaviors. Students were not only disruptive in class but they also were at times violent with each other. Their principal took decisive action and invested in a three-week restorative justice training for all the teachers that also included ongoing push in support throughout the year. The results were amazing for students, teachers, and families. Inspired by the progress, another school in the district also shifted to restorative justice. At the time, they couldn't invest in the training and instead just implemented circles and ended their Saturday detention program. Their results weren't so favorable. Teachers felt that students were not held accountable, there was not enough time in the day to run all the circles, and families complained when their students were hurt or affected and administrators did "nothing."

Any system that a school or classroom adopts comes with the tangible reality and constraints of the school day. Restorative justice might not have the immediate and familiar look of punishments such as missing recess or detention, but with the proper time and dedication, it can be successful. When teachers are highly trained in the methods and mindsets that undergird restorative justice and honor the roots and legacy of the practices, magic can happen.

Mindset Shift 20: Understanding Harm

When a student acts out or exhibits a negative behavior, what do you do? Most teachers will either look for a consequence, a punishment, or find some way to hold them accountable. But does that mean they addressed the harm caused by the behavior? Consider this example:

A sneaky student, let's call them Jordan, takes another student's color pencils from home and uses them while they're doing center rotations. Jordan ends up breaking some of the pencils.

Here are some things to think about in the teacher response:

The teacher responds by telling Jordan that they will miss their recess because it's against the classroom norms to use others' materials. (punishment)

The teacher responds by telling Jordan that he has to give *his* color pencils to the other student—and Jordan won't be able to use any colored pencils for the rest of the day. (consequence)

But do these address the harm that was done? A student had some of their colored pencils broken; that is a form of harm and needs to be put right.

When I was in my first year of teaching middle school, I worked with a truly diverse mix of students—and there were often racial tensions among them. These kids were dealing with their own identity and maturation while trying to make sense of the world as social media became more and more ubiquitous. More than once inappropriate phrases were exchanged, whether they were phrases that they picked up from TikTok, or outright racial or misogynistic slurs, it felt like I was constantly responding to language.

Sometimes we punished the students for their language infraction—like give them detention. When the target of such language was one of my identities—as a Black woman—that's what I wanted to do! I wanted them to sit at school until 6 p.m. because they used a racial slur about Black people. I was hurt by the comments, the other Black kids were hurt by the comments, I wanted the student to feel bad, too.

Sometimes we focused on consequences—something that made sense and was a logical response to the situation. For example, they'd have to stay in during a free period, but the time would be spent learning about why the words they used were so problematic.

But what neither of these solutions did was address the harm that was caused. When the students on the receiving end of those barbed words heard them coming from a classmate it caused them harm. It was hurtful and painful. And it was hurtful and painful to me as their teacher. Addressing harm is a critical piece of being restorative and holding the student accountable, because they were not only accountable for their actions but also how they made others feel.

When you're thinking about a response to student behavior it's critical that you consider how to address harm. Whether a student is causing harm to an individual or the classroom community, understanding harm and having empathy for people that you've harmed will lead to a caring classroom community that functions well without you having to just manage students.

I've found that harm is a much more effective way for students and families to understand the implications of their behavior. In my first year of teaching, I fell back on "it's a rule" and "because I said so" type of reasoning. This does not always resonate with students or families. If they don't see the inherent value in the rule, they are not going to support you and help you hold the student accountable. When instead you focus on harm caused and the way that a students' actions impacts others, it is easier for everyone to understand.

To build a joyful and inclusive classroom ecosystem, students have care about harming each other, not just about following rules.

EQUITY/RACISM/SOCIAL JUSTICE

We can't fully understand what it means to build a classroom culture rooted in joy, inclusion, care, and belonging without first looking at what makes it so difficult in the first place. Schools and teachers are not immune to the -isms and injustices of society. We must grapple with the legacy of oppression, bias, and inequity in our schools before we can imagine and build something better.

Mindset Shift 21: Bias and Behavior

If you go into a typical school or classroom across the country, you'll probably hear something about respect.

Respect others, respect your teachers, adults—whatever it is, respect is a concept that we frequently teach students as a golden rule. But when you get right down to it, what does it mean to show respect or be respectful? If you ask different students and adults you'll probably get different answers.

Much of it is about culture. Different cultures have different ideas and perspectives about what it means to be respectful and, perhaps more important, what it means to be disrespectful. Let's just think about going into someone else's home, for example.

First, if you weren't invited, is it disrespectful to invite yourself over? If you were invited, should you call before you arrive? Should you arrive right on time—or does your host expect you to be a little late?

When you enter the house, do you take your shoes off? Do you bring a gift or dish to share? Should you offer to help? If you enjoy the food is it okay to get seconds? Will you know when it's time to leave?

As you were reading this scenario you probably had all kinds of thoughts and reactions. Moments when you thought "of course!" or "no way!" but there really isn't one right or wrong answer. You see, respect isn't really all that objective. But in too many classrooms it's treated that way—and that's one of the many reasons why we end up with so much inequity in our classrooms.

One study looked at what teachers were most frequently referring students for and what types of behaviors they were most commonly punished for. The teachers in the study did not share a racial and cultural identity with their students, which is a critical element to understand because we can infer that perhaps there were different ideas of respect for each party. The researchers looked at the data to examine what were the most common behaviors. The findings were fascinating. The teachers more frequently cited the Black and Brown students for more subjective and less narrowly defined behaviors such as disrespect.

Respect is just one part of the story. Bias shows up in many different responses to behavior.

So, are Black and Brown students just poorly behaved? Well, consider the finding of the following study. Some teachers were asked to monitor a group of students and look for behaviors, but what the study was actually doing was monitoring teacher eye movements. The researchers wanted to see which students were being watched the most—and, sure enough, the Black students were being watched more, which, of course, led to more behaviors getting noticed (Healy, 2016).

Another study looked at the responses teachers had to particular behaviors and found that, even if two students have the same behavior—say, talking out of turn, fighting at school, or maybe not following expectations or rules at recess—Black and Brown students received harsher consequences for the same behavior (Riddle & Sinclair, 2019)!

Additionally in 2017, Georgetown produced a critical study on girls that showed that they were often "adultified" at school—meaning they were perceived as older and less deserving of the empathy, care, and tenderness you'd use with a child (Epstein et al., n.d.).

Why? It's complex, but it definitely has to do with racism. Not the violent, extreme racism that you're used to seeing in black-and-white photos from the 1960s, but a much more salient and surreptitious form of racism. Teachers are perfectly willing to teach Black and Brown students—they just have lower expectations and harsher punishments for those students than they do for their white students.

Sometimes it's labeled as a *bias* or a *microaggression*, but it's the fruit of the same tree that grows racism. Because it goes by so many other names sometimes the impact and severity of the problem can get obscured, but whether it's clear on the surface, such as segregation, or it is insidious, such as inequitable practices in enrollment, the impact is still here. What can make this even more dangerous is many teachers aren't even aware that they are carrying these biases.

Think back to the teachers you've worked with throughout your career and any inequity you might have seen at different schools. Whether it was a certain type of student always getting in trouble, or over-enrollment of a particular demographic in SPED, you probably didn't see too much blatant racism. But that doesn't mean that teachers weren't operating from positions of bias. Despite the good intentions and friendly interpersonal interactions, institutional and systemic racism is still pervasive in education.

But that's why it's so important to understand anti-racism. Consider this analogy: the history of the United States and 400 years of systemic racism means that the institutions themselves are racist. It's not just education. Whether it's the racism in the health care field, where Black and Latinx patients receive lower quality of care in 40% of the metrics used by the US Department of Health according to their 2020 report. Or housing, where the practice of redlining meant Black people were either unable to secure loans in certain areas or had their home severely undervalued (Jackson, 2021). And if we learned one thing from 2020 it's that the US criminal justice system is deeply rooted in racism.

In her book *Why Are All the Black Kids Sitting Together in the Cafeteria?* Dr. Beverly Daniel Tatum offers an intriguing conceptualization of racism:

> I sometimes visualize the ongoing cycle of racism as a moving walkway at the airport. Active racist behavior is equivalent to walking fast on the conveyor belt. The person engaged in active racist behavior has identified with the ideology of White supremacy and is moving with it.
>
> Passive racist behavior is equivalent to standing still on the walkway. No overt effort is being made, but the conveyor belt moves the bystanders along to the same destination as those who are actively walking. Some of the bystanders may feel the motion of the conveyor belt, see the active racists ahead of them, and choose to turn around, unwilling to go in the same destination as the White supremacists. But unless they are walking actively in the opposite direction at a speed faster than the conveyor belt—unless they are actively anti-racist—they will find themselves carried along with the others. (Tatum, 2017 p. 91)

In this country, we're all standing on that walkway, and it's taking us in the direction of racism. So being still—the default, doing nothing—isn't enough, because racism is so deeply ingrained in our systems. So when we think about anti-racism, it isn't about not being racist, it's about being actively anti-racist—running the opposite way on the moving walkway.

So where do teachers fit in to all this?

We start with awareness. For example, most teachers think about the way that they treat their Black and Brown students as evidence that they are not racist. But it's not always about just being nice or even kind. Even if you look at so-called neutral curriculums, there is racism. For example, some stories are left out in Social Studies. In the wake of the anti-CRT movement, schools are going as far as removing the "Letter from Birmingham Jail" written by Dr. Martin Luther King Jr. and books on the movement to desegregate schools (Stinson, 2021). Until a recent movement about #representationmatters, our libraries were disproportionately filled with stories of white students. So, although we've made progress, we still have a long way to go.

When it comes to behavior specifically, the system is designed to work against Black and Brown kids, as we see in the data that show them disproportionately disciplined, suspended, and expelled as young as pre-K. So teachers themselves may not be actively racist, but we have to address (and work against!) institutional racism in our schools.

It's not just enough to be aware. Teachers can certainly get active in local politics, become informed voters, and find other ways to disrupt systemic racism. But you can start with the classroom space. By becoming aware of your bias, and then building a classroom ecosystem that is rooted in joy, belonging, and care, instead of systemic racism, you are slowly but surely headed in the right direction on the moving walkway.

What Does Culture Have to Do with Behavior?

There are many ways we differ between cultures. For instance, some cultures consider it acceptable to talk over each other (called *cooperative overlap*). In some cultures, it would be acceptable to joke with your teacher. Some cultures also have an inherent deference to authority, and others do not. Figure 3.2 presents some common impacts.

Figure 3.2 Behavior Derives from Culture

Mindset Shift 22: Big Behaviors Also Need an Asset-Based Lens

I once worked at a middle school that prided itself on equity. And yet, when it came down to making decisions about how to respond to big behaviors—the kind that can do some serious harm—equity was the first thing we scrapped. Students were destroying school property, skipping classes, and getting close to physical altercations with each other. The behaviors were reaching a crescendo and we were running out of ideas of how to respond.

We didn't know how to move forward, so we decided to try out more punitive measures: missing recess, after-school detention, Saturday school, and suspension.

Taking away recess didn't work. Because the students didn't get a chance to decompress, they ended up being even more disruptive. The other punishments weren't effective for many reasons, but, primarily, the punishments perpetuated the same systems of harm that we sought to combat. Detention is a carceral practice, just like suspension and expulsion are. Nothing worked.

We *talked* about equity, representation, and diversity. The students had affinity groups and curricular materials that they felt represented by. All our equity work, however, stopped when it was time to think about how to react to behavior. Schools across the country find themselves in this same position: thinking about equity in an instructional sense, but not yet reflecting on what it means to be equitable, trauma informed, or even culturally responsive with how you respond to behavior challenges. We use an equity and anti-racist lens in our proactive conversations, but not in our reactive conversations. We need both.

What if we had responded with an asset-based approach? What if we got creative? What if we thought about what our students were doing well and found a way to tap in to that? What if we stepped back and looked at the overall health of our school community? Or asked what the behaviors were telling us?

Teachers employ many different systems to support students in their day-by-day, hour-by-hour ups and downs. You might use a check-in system. Maybe students are accruing time to spend in free choice or working toward extra recess time. Maybe you have community agreements and when students don't follow those agreements you have a meeting or family conference. But it's the big behaviors that expose the most inequity. When the big challenges arise, don't walk away from your commitment to asset-based behavior responses.

Mindset Shift 23: Classroom Management or the School-to-Prison Pipeline?

Sometimes it's difficult to see the broader implications of the small decisions we make in the classroom. After all, you're just one teacher. It's just one day; it's just one recess. Just one suspension. But it's critical that we understand that our actions as individuals can contribute to larger systemic issues.

An equity issue that has been detailed by several scholars such as Michelle Alexander, Monique Morris, and David Stovall is the school-to-prison pipeline or the school-to-prison nexus, where schools, along with other entities such as social service organizations, funnel Black and Brown kids from schools into the prison system. These systems work together and are intentionally designed to feed into each other. Students who are referred to school resource officers, for example, can be arrested and sent to either juvenile detention facilities or continuation schools. When students are no longer in the traditional school setting, their options are limited. They won't have access to AP classes or other accelerated courses that put them on the path to thrive instead of just survive (ACLU, 2020).

But what does behavior management have to do with prisons? First a few statistics:

- Black and brown kids are overrepresented in SPED (NCLD, 2020).
- More than half of the kids and eventual adults in the criminal justice system report some kind of neurodivergence or learning difference (U.S. Department of Justice, 2016).
- Of all incarcerated people 70% read below a 4th-grade reading level (U.S. Department of Justice, 2016).

How do these systems interact? Consider an all-too familiar scenario: a student is disruptive in class. Let's say this student is bothering others, refusing to sit in their seat, and the teacher has less than 15 minutes to review critical information before a test the next day. The teacher kicks the student out of class, or maybe they send them to the principal's office. If this is a regular issue for the student, they might end up qualifying for additional services, or worst-case scenario be labeled with something like oppositional defiance disorder. Even if the student isn't eligible for additional services, they might develop a reputation and record of bad behavior at the school. Some schools have strict policies such as zero tolerance that require suspensions or expulsions. Ultimately, the school is responsible for ensuring the safety of their students, so removing a student from a situation is sometimes necessary, but the more time the student spends out of school, the further they fall behind, and they begin to exhibit work-avoidant behaviors, such as being disruptive, which ends up in them spending even less time in class.

This cycle can lead to many different negative outcomes: the student could get suspended too frequently and end up being referred to social services, even removed from their home. The student could eventually be expelled from the local school and referred to an alternative school or credit recovery. These schools have a graduation rate of only about 40% (PACE, 2018). Not graduating high school significantly increases your likelihood of being incarcerated (Camera, 2021).

Far too many students fall into this pipeline. There are valid reasons why a student might need to take a break from class. But as educators we cannot ignore the role that schools have played in perpetuating inequity. Classroom management absolutely is a part of the school-to-prison pipeline.

In the moment, it feels like just one decision to send a student out, but when you look at the broader system at play, it can be something much bigger.

Mindset Shift 24: Understanding White Supremacy Culture

This is a big one. And it's important. You may already have an understanding of white supremacy culture, but it's important that we name white supremacy culture in the classroom.

According to the National Education Association's Center for Social Justice (2020), "white supremacy is a form of racism centered upon the belief that white people are superior to people of other racial backgrounds and that whites should politically, economically, and socially dominate non-whites. While often associated with violence perpetuated by the KKK and other white supremacist groups, it also describes a political ideology and systemic oppression that perpetuates and maintains the social, political, historical and or/industrial white domination."

White supremacy culture, essentially, is the idea that white ideologies, behaviors, and beliefs are superior to the ideologies, behaviors, and beliefs of people of color. This isn't about how individual white people feel about individual people of color. This is not to be confused with the more violent white supremacy movements that have been popping up across the United States at an alarming rate. It's about systems in the United States that are undergirded by the idea that whiteness is better or normal. Do you see white supremacy culture show up at your school? If you said no, look a little closer. In many schools, white supremacy looks like white just being the default. Normal. Average. That is, anything related to other cultures is something extra. Let's look at a few examples.

When you went to college, or maybe even in high school, there were probably electives that you could take on Asian cultures, Black culture, or Latinx cultures, but those were electives. The expectation was that your baseline, what you had to study, was European history and culture. The school might have talked about other stories, but they were probably in relation to how these cultures affected Europeans.

When you heard stories about other cultures in school, was it from the perspective of white Europeans? Did it intentionally paint Europeans in a neutral or positive light regardless of whether they were right or wrong in the situation? For example, were Europeans "exploring" or "discovering" the "New World"? Or where they colonizing and engaging in cultural genocide?

This also shows up in language. Each state has different laws or protocols for how they deal with newcomers—students who have recently arrived in the United States and students who speak a language other than English at home. Some call them *Els* or *English learners* or *emergent bilinguals*—whatever the phrasing, schools and districts have set policies in place for how to accommodate these students. Too often I've seen these students over-enrolled in speech and language services or enrolled in ELL classes, which are essentially classes to help them formalize their English skills. On a practical level, this makes sense. Learning formal English eliminates barriers in other classes that require English fluency. But many schools hold these classes during elective time or lock students out of other opportunities and spaces because they are not designated as English proficient. English is necessary to navigate most schools, but how many students miss out on opportunities because they're automatically devalued for not speaking perfect, formal English?

When you look at a school calendar, what days are accommodated for? Although it's true that not everyone who honors the Gregorian calendar or celebrates Christian holidays is white, the school calendar is still largely shaped around holidays that have held high value for white Americans.

This isn't a book about white supremacy culture, but it's important that we look at how some of the characteristics of white supremacy culture are showing up in our classroom. You should absolutely invest time and energy into learning more about white supremacy culture and its larger implications.

Remember, noticing white supremacy culture around you doesn't mean you are a white supremacist. You can participate and perpetuate white supremacy culture and have Black and Brown friends and relatives. You can even perpetuate white supremacy culture and be a person of color. It's just like the moving walkway of racism.

All education stakeholders could benefit from learning more about white supremacy culture. In 2001 Kenneth Jones and Tema Okun outlined a list of characteristics of white supremacy culture and how they show up in organizations. Here are just a few of the characteristics of white supremacy culture and how they show up in our classroom:

Perfectionism is a deficit approach that hyper-focuses on shortcomings and inadequacies. When a mistake is made it's viewed as a personal failing instead of just a mistake.

In the classroom this looks like focusing on negative student behaviors and identifying "difficult" students or "troublemakers." Instead of acknowledging that all kids show up in different ways and that we should encourage all of them to thrive, we reduce them to their behaviors and label them as "good" or "bad."

Quantity over quality is the focus on measurable goals and things that can be quantified prevailing over care and the quality of interactions.

In the classroom this looks like a hyper-focus on schedules, timing and process without stopping to ensure that your students are emotionally well.

Only one right way is a belief that there is only one right way to do things. If someone doesn't adapt to the change, they are wrong.

In the classroom this looks like having one way of doing things. One process. One way of being. This is particularly detrimental for neurodivergent students who have many different ways of interacting with their surroundings.

We see this with students of color as well. If the teacher has established a way to sit, move about the room, or any way of being that is based on their own cultural values, then students who don't follow that are "wrong."

Paternalism is when people who hold power believe that they can make decisions about what's best for people who are not in power.

In the classroom it can look like classroom cultures that are created by the teacher without the input, consideration, and ideas from the students. It also looks like decision-making processes for communities about what needs the school should address without the involvement of said community.

Individualism is hyper-focus on individual actors and actions, instead of community.

In the classroom this looks like teachers fostering the mindset that students only have an obligation to themselves, not their classroom community, and that individual success is more important than collective progress.

Objectivity is the false consciousness that we can be truly objective or neutral.

In the classroom this looks like seeing certain behaviors or systems as objective and therefore not racist, heterocentric, ableist, misogynistic, and so on. It can look like teachers refusing to acknowledge the impact of white supremacy culture and instead insisting that their cultural frame of reference is "normal," "obvious," or "common sense." (For more, see Tema Okun's website, https://www.whitesupremacyculture.info/.)

It is critical that teachers recognize white supremacy culture in schools and in their classrooms because then we can move away from problematizing the students and instead problematize the systems. For example, for decades teachers, thought leaders, and politicians alike have invested time and money in closing the "achievement gap," the statistical trend where Black and Latinx students perform lower on standardized tests than their white counterparts. The numbers are staggering. In California, for example, less than one-third of 3rd graders are at or above grade level in reading, and that was before the 2020 COVID-19 pandemic (Fensterwald, 2022). Black, Latinx, and Indigenous high schoolers are less likely to be in AP classes and make it to and through four-year colleges. At some point it begs the question, what if it's not the kids? What if it's the metrics? If the metrics that we use to measure Black and Brown children are rooted in white supremacy culture, then we can't be surprised if they are found lacking.

Committing to this work does not mean that you are dedicated to helping Black and Brown students do better by white metrics and standards. It's time for a new rubric.

When you think about the classroom and the classroom culture strategy, too many of us are focused on finding creative and fun ways to incentivize performing whiteness because that's what good behavior looks like. We need to accept that standards of behavior have been influenced by white supremacy culture, so our goal post has to change.

But what if our classroom is all white students? We are not all affected by white supremacy culture in the same way, but still we are all affected. Narrow ideas of what good and bad behavior look like are harmful to us all. White supremacy culture is also rooted in patriarchy and neurotypicality, which means it can very much harm white students as well.

So what does this all mean?

When I work with teachers sometimes they don't understand the ideological shift that has to come along with asset and liberatory pedagogies such as anti-racism, culturally responsive teaching, or abolitionist teaching. If you don't shift your mindset, you won't be successful.

For example, I led a workshop on some implementable strategies in October 2021. We talked about white supremacy culture, practices for the classroom, and even did some role-playing. I often include a follow-up session for schools, because it's one thing to hear something in a PD setting but it's another to actually have to put it in practice. I came for the follow-up a few months later. Overall, the teachers were excited about the new strategies, but they still had some remaining questions. One teacher in particular was still very frustrated.

"I did everything you said. I've been doing more circles and talking with parents more, but I still have a student who likes to get out of his chair and wander around while I'm talking. He's gotten better, but he still does it at least once a week."

I get it. It used to throw me off when students did this. I got distracted. I panicked that they weren't listening. I used all of my carrots and sticks to try to get them to comply. But then I stepped back. He wasn't bothering other students. I actually had no idea if he was listening or not. I just wanted him to be in his chair because that's what a "good" student looked like. Sometimes there's a really good reason why kids should be sitting down. Sometimes there's not. It's absolutely critical that we know the difference.

I told her about my experience. Then I told her lovingly that I think she may want to revisit our mindset work. Asset-based practices in the classroom cannot and will not help you force your students into complying with white supremacy culture. If fact, if they did then they wouldn't be working.

Instead the goal is to shift the focus away from compliance and instead to community. Away from individual failings and success and into community health. To let go of the idea that a good classroom culture looks like students sitting exactly where we want them to for six or more hours a day.

We must change our rubrics and measurements of success and realize that our students are whole, human people whom we seek to learn with and build communities for, not control.

When students are forced to comply with white supremacy culture in their classrooms, they can't experience the true joy of being the fullest versions of themselves.

Mindset Shift 25: If You Treat Kids Like Criminals, They'll Act Like Criminals

This may come as a shock to lower elementary teachers or teachers in more quiet areas, but there are students across this country who are policed at school; they even go through metal detectors and are searched when they enter their school buildings. Almost 50% of schools report having a police officer on campus (Sawchuk, 2021). This is most common in high school, but it's not unheard of in lower grades, too. Schools will claim that these measures exist to keep kids safe, but when we look at the data, the schools *without* the carceral measures such as police officers and metal detectors are typically the most safe. Criminalizing students takes a mental and emotional toll on students. Black, Indigenous, and Latinx boys and girls are up to four times more likely to be suspended or expelled, but they're also more likely to be restrained at school as well (Lewin, 2012; Reuters Staff, 2016; NCLD, 2020). Now more than ever we understand that systemic racism thrives in the criminal justice system. We must consider how continuing to link education and police affects our Black and Brown students who are disproportionally murdered by them.

There are countless instances of schools calling the police on students with disastrous results. In Philadelphia, a 3rd grader was removed by a police officer for refusing to stop talking during art class. In 2019 a student missed several months of school due to fighting a disorderly conduct charge following an altercation with the school police. The student apparently refused to surrender his cell phone and was arrested. In 2020, a Maryland kindergartener was put in handcuffs after refusing to comply with a teacher's directions. A 14-year-old student was tased in Minneapolis after she refused to comply with an officer's orders. These are just a few of the many stories about school police (Hacker et al., 2022). In schools like these, can students really feel safe? Can they feel like they belong?

In some schools, the student body might actually feel more safe with school police and metal detectors, but the data don't show that these schools are actually safer. Even with the shameful and dark history of school shootings in the United States, we've seen in several instances that the presence of a school police officer doesn't necessarily make kids less likely to be killed at school or any safer. Students who are tased, arrested, and otherwise harassed by police at school can certainly be traumatized by the interaction. Other student who witness police violence against their classmates may also be traumatized and begin to feel unsafe or afraid at school.

What if we invest those resources into building school communities? What if the personnel funds that go to school police officers went to school social workers or therapists? How we decide to allocate funds sends a message to our students. What message do we send when we underfund the arts and social emotional health in lieu of school police?

Teachers have very tangible and valid concerns for their safety. Unfortunately, underfunded schools, overburdened mental health professionals, and poor school leadership have culminated in a surge of dangerous student behavior. The solution, however, is not to criminalize our students, but instead to take a long, hard look at how our schools are failing them.

SOME TRUTHS ABOUT TRAUMA

Typically, when we talk about seeing the whole student we focus on understanding the contextual factors that might be affecting how that student shows up to our classrooms. It is critical to see that students are bringing their experiences to the table—and our kids experience a lot, as much as many adults experience. We are all navigating a world that is unfortunately steeped in systems of oppression. If you work in classrooms long enough, you'll hear story after story about difficult home lives, immigration challenges, death, abuse, you name it—but our kids' stories don't stop there. Students are more than just a compilation of all the bad things that have ever happened to them. There's a fine line between pathologizing our students and being mindful of their experiences.

Mindset Shift 26: Our Kids Are More Than Their Trauma

Sometimes schools ask me to host workshops on trauma-informed care. Although I am not an expert in the subject, I have helped many schools and teachers incorporate trauma-informed practices into their pedagogy. I always start off a workshop asking what different types of trauma their students are experiencing. I commonly get answers about racism, domestic violence, poverty, single-adult households, or housing insecurity. Many teachers share with me the heartbreaking challenges that their students are experiencing at home. And, of course, trauma affects us both emotionally and physically.

But sometimes teachers get stuck in a sentimentalist mindset. In her 2014 book *Culturally Responsive Teaching and the Brain: Promoting Authentic Engagement and Rigor Among*

Culturally and Linguistically Diverse Students, Zaretta Hammond describes the sentimentalist as the teacher who is focused on relationship building but holds low expectations for their students out of pity. (Hammond is expanding on Judith Kleinfeld, who in 1975 coined the term *warm demander* to describe teachers who build strong relationships with their students while having high expectations of them.) The sentimentalists are teachers who are only seeing students as a summation of their trauma. When you have close relationships with students and families, you might start to experience this. Some of our students are at the intersection of multiple forms of systemic oppression. The more you learn about their experiences, the easier it is to exclusively reduce students to their trauma.

Some teachers under the guise of a "trauma-informed" or "culturally responsive" lens lower their expectations for students and get wrapped up in a cycle of pity and patronization. When you only see the deficits in your students—their trauma, how hard it must be at home for them, how many odds are stacked up against them—you miss critical opportunities to help them build their own agency. This mindset of pity doesn't help students thrive.

Shawn Ginwright offers healing-centered pedagogy as a framework that can perhaps help teachers see the nuance in responding to students who have experienced trauma. Instead of focusing on only trauma, healing-centered engagement centers on well-being and the restoration of identity. Students explore their own purpose, identity, and self-compassion. Healing-centered pedagogy also acknowledges that adults themselves can need healing. As opposed to a model where the students are the "healed" and adults are the "healers," both sides work together to build connections with each other and themselves (Ginwright, 2018).

When you look at your students, see all of their experiences and remember that they are complex and dynamic—and much more than their trauma.

Mindset Shift 27: Schools Can Be Traumatic, Too

Trauma doesn't only happen at home. Many students—particularly our Black, Indigenous, and other students of color—need healing from the trauma they experience at school.

Recently the study of epigenetics and a deeper understanding of biology has shed light on the fact that our bodies do indeed have a physical response to racism and oppression. Several studies of telomeres, the protective endcaps of chromosomes, have suggested that premature shortening of telomeres causes cells to age early. What causes this? Well, at least one cause is racism. The systemic racism that students experience at school matters. The social pressures that kids experience on a daily basis navigating systems of oppression greatly affects both their mental health and their physical health (Watson, 2019). Many teachers would say that standardized testing can be a traumatic experience for students. In many districts kids spend weeks in standardized testing. These high-stakes tests are demoralizing for many students. They spend hours sitting through these tests that are rarely implemented to support student learning (Berwick, 2019).

And then there's the trauma that students experience when they're suspended and/or expelled from school. As educators we must be honest and realistic about the cumulative trauma that our kids might be experiencing in our buildings.

Mindset Shift 28: Families Are Struggling, Too

As a school leader and teacher, there were many days when I was extremely frustrated about parents missing my calls, missing conferences, or what I perceived as apathy. It's easy to say parents just don't care—and to judge or even condemn them as caregivers. But the truth and reality are much more complex. Sometimes you have to take a step back and realize that the adults may be doing their best—they may simply not have enough capacity to show up how we want or need them to.

The Bureau of Labor Statistics estimates that, in the average two-adult household, parents have less than one hour during the weekday to spend relaxing and socializing with their child outside of domestic duties. In single-earner or single-caregiver households, or when the parent works more than one job, the children get even less time (U.S. Bureau of Labor Statistics, 2021).

And don't forget that that trauma is equally experienced by their caregivers. Even families who don't experience the challenges of systemic oppression are still dealing with the stress of entrusting their children for many hours every day to people who are essentially strangers. Many of the challenges with caregivers come down to trust. If they don't trust you, they'll have a difficult time seeing that you're on the same team. Families also might not fully comprehend or understand the complexities of running a classroom—not to mention the dramatic shifts in the educational landscape post COVID-19.

Families can be our biggest assets and allies in this work. It's critical to extend grace and have patience with them.

Mindset Shift 29: Teaching After COVID

Many aspects of educational practices come and go in pendulum swings and cycles—trends about what works go in and out of fashion. But COVID-19 has changed a lot about teaching—some practices may be permanently changed.

We have to address the elephant in the room: kids come to the classroom with more baggage and trauma than ever before. The following details just some of the changes our kids are experiencing:

- A national survey found that more than 50% of students reported more trouble completing their school work and emotional distress at home post-2020 (Krause et al., 2021).
- Previously, the general rule for understanding a child's attention span was to double their age in minutes—meaning that a six-year-old would have around a 12-minute attention span. Research is beginning to suggest, and anecdotal data from teachers are confirming, that many students are suffering reduced attention spans after the pandemic (Maryam, 2022).
- Some students have spent their first three years of school in pandemic schooling. That will certainly affect their attention span, their understanding of being in community with others, and their stamina in general.
- There have also been several studies on mental health that suggest that the pandemic took its toll on adults and kids alike, leading the American Psychology Association to declare a children's mental health crisis (Abramson, 2022).

Teaching has changed. It is absolutely necessary for school leaders and policy makers to make teaching more sustainable. This would start with the much-needed shifts of paying teachers more, lowering class sizes, and providing more funding for mental health support. But even with those measures, teaching may never be the same as it was before the pandemic. What does that mean for behavior and classroom culture?

It means that the methods that served us before the pandemic might not directly translate to post-pandemic life. It means that now, more than ever, we have no choice but to consider the social-emotional weight that our students bring into the classroom. We have to find new ways of building community and new ways of schooling.

CHAPTER 4

Building a Healthy Ecosystem

There's an old legend that sometimes gets attributed to the Lenape people. You might have heard it before, but perhaps not in the context of teaching. A grandfather tells his grandson: "There are two wolves within. One is focused on revenge, anger, and negativity. The other one is focused on joy, light, and positivity." When the grandson asks which one wins, the grandpa responds, "Whichever one you feed."

You can apply this same logic to the classroom culture. If you invest all your time and energy into what to do when something goes wrong, how you will respond to negative behavior, and how to punish students, the negativity will win. Your approach will be centered on the challenges in the classroom and how to respond to them.

But if you anchor the classroom in positivity and focus on building joy and community, the positivity will win. Instead you'll build a toolbox of practices that help your students feel joyful, cared for, and a sense of belonging.

It's not easy. There will be challenges, and you do have to be able to respond to your students when their behaviors arise, but your overall experience and your students' experience of your room is largely determined by which wolf you feed. Where will you invest your energy?

CLASSROOMS ARE ECOSYSTEMS

We often talk about classrooms and use the term *communities*. That makes sense: the classroom is a small community of folks working together for a common goal (even when it doesn't seem like it!). The ideal vision for the classroom is that everyone is working together to learn.

But the classroom isn't just a community—it's an ecosystem. A classroom is a complex web of interdependent relationships and connections that ideally can thrive together. And just as the biological ecosystems that we teach children about can be healthy or unhealthy ecosystems, the same applies to classroom ecosystems.

In a healthy classroom ecosystem, the components are in right relationship with each other. That doesn't mean that there are no challenges, but it does mean that there are systems in place to work through challenges and move forward.

In an unhealthy ecosystem, the components are not in right relationship. There are imbalances and inequities. And because all of the elements are interrelated, what start out as small challenges between a few members can grow into bigger, even community-wide problems. Even just one student can dramatically shift the energy in a classroom and affect what all the other students experience. And, unfortunately, a classroom with a few highly dysregulated students can get stuck in an unhealthy cycle with no way to get back on track.

I like to think about ecosystems specifically for a few reasons:

Ecosystems are dependent on their physical environment. The classroom is more than just the students; it's how the desks are arranged, where everyone sits, what goes where, and the flow of the entire space.

Ecosystems are highly interdependent. The choices and behaviors of each individual affect the whole. All teachers know, for example, that the personalities and actions of one student can influence the entire classroom.

Ecosystems are unique. What works in the classroom down the hall might not work for you. A desert ecosystem is not the same as a rainforest, but both can find their own cadence and function appropriately in their setting.

Ecosystems are not stagnant. This might be the most critical parallel between classrooms and ecosystems. They change, grow, and develop. The classroom culture is not something that you can let blossom on standby. In fact, when the teacher does not clearly codesign an ecosystem with students, the students create their own. And you don't need me to tell you the systems they create aren't always inclusive, joyful, or productive.

Take a minute to envision what your ideal classroom ecosystem could look like.

- What does it feel like to be in the classroom?
- What does it sound like?
- How do the students feel?
- How do you feel?
- How is everything organized?
- What do the students experience each day?
- How does the ecosystem respond when there's a problem?

The ecosystem is really just a web of relationships, and the classroom is no different.

Ecosystems Are Relationships

Is it your job to build relationships with your students? In short, yes. Even if it's not in your contract, it's in your best interest. And I say that knowing full well how chronically overburdened teachers are. Teachers' workloads are one of the primary reasons this country has a teacher turnover problem. According to *Edweek*, after five years only about one-third of the teachers who entered the field will still be teaching (Loewus, 2021). Current expectations of teachers are just not sustainable. Everyone has a limited bandwidth. When your bandwidth is low, you might feel you don't have the energy to build relationships. But that doesn't change the facts that, first, the classroom is an ecosystem, and, second, an ecosystem is really just a web of relationships. Healthy classroom ecosystems are founded on relationships, and strong teacher-student relationships can make all the difference. Relationships should be the absolute last thing to go.

If you spend time in the first month building relationships with students and laying the foundation for a healthy classroom culture, your work will certainly pay off. If you jump into the year without laying that foundation, you'll likely be playing catch-up for the rest of the year.

The reason for this is that students respond better when they feel that their teachers are invested in them. So when a challenge arises with a student, or with several students, your relationship with those students could be what leads to a de-escalation—instead of a classroom crisis that leads to one or more kids getting suspended.

Teachers understand this at a human level as well. I once worked with a school leader who was absolutely beloved by the teachers. He was great about building relationships. He knew birthdays, kid's names, and always had snacks in his office. He was direct and had high expectations of his teachers, but he also had authentic and substantive relationships with each and every one of them. He semiretired and we got a new principal. She was actually more flexible with deadlines, dress code, and expectations, but the teachers just didn't receive her the same way. She didn't take time to get to know us. We didn't feel like she was invested in us or our kids. So when she'd give feedback to teachers, they were less open to it because they felt like she didn't really understand what they were experiencing.

In 2013, Rita Pierson presented a TED Talk that has amassed more than 5.5 million views. In it, she tells us that "every kid needs a champion." If you haven't seen the video, it's worth a watch. She speaks about the power of relationships with students and how "kids don't learn from people they don't like." She explains that students need to feel like their teachers like and care about them. Does that mean that you have to like every child? To again quote the late great Rita Pierson, "Of course not!"

But that does mean that you'll need to put effort into getting to know your students. Some of them will come to you, and it'll be easy and effortless. For other students it'll be like pulling teeth. But *all* students need a connection with their teachers. You don't have to be everyone's favorite teacher; you just have to be present and engaged and demonstrate to each student that they have a place in the classroom.

And there's a huge plus side to this: the relationship-building piece can be the most fun! There will be days when your relationships with students will be *the* thing that gets you through the day. This can be the joyful part.

Have a little fun with your students. Let your personality out and be your authentic self. The relationships you build with students can be restorative and can actually replenish your energy and spirit if you let it.

An Effective Teacher Is an Authentic Teacher

Relationships don't mean that every student loves you all the time. In fact, if you aren't lovingly pushing your students to be the best versions of themselves each day then you aren't really building a relationship with them. It can be challenging at first to navigate those moments when you don't feel liked by your students. Especially if you are a people-pleaser personality type. Students absolutely want to feel connected with their teachers and get a sense of warmth and even humor from them, but there will be times when building relationships with students means helping them through difficult situations or holding them accountable with love.

Some teachers are overly concerned or anxious about not being liked by students and it ends up harming them in the long term. For example, a teacher I worked with, Mr. Lee, with had an instant and warm connection with one of his 7th graders, Javier. I think Mr. Lee probably felt like he was like Javier when he was at that age. His intentions weren't all bad, but Javier absolutely took advantage of this connection. Mr. Lee was so worried about being disliked by Javier that he turned a blind eye to some of his inappropriate comments and behaviors in the classroom. This culminated in a very serious cyberbullying incident involving some other students. Mr. Lee admitted that there were signs and moments that he should have called Javier into a conversation about accountability. He was worried that by holding Javier accountable that he'd lose the relationship. It might be true that Javier would be frustrated by Mr. Lee's decision to hold him accountable, but ultimately the classroom community suffered. In an effort to make Javier like him, Mr. Lee made it difficult for the other students to find a sense of belonging in the classroom.

Focus on building authentic, warm, and consistent connections with students, instead of trying to befriend them. Did anyone else learn "don't smile until Christmas" in their teacher preparation program? I'm not sure if my professor was serious, but they told us, especially the middle school teachers, that we'd need this advice once we got into the classroom. I don't think that's the answer either. It can be especially difficult for new, young teachers to find the line between being relatable and having boundaries.

When new teachers (and veteran teachers, too!) don't know how to navigate professionalism and boundaries with their students, they can go into what I call lock-down mode. They give very few details, no pictures showing their families, no opportunities for the kids to ask questions, they're all business. I do want to note here that, unfortunately, some teachers have no choice but to hide certain aspects of their identities from their students and their school community. This is unacceptable and a disgrace to every district with these policies in place. This isn't about those teachers. Rather, here I'm referring to the teachers that actively chose to create distance from their students because they subscribe to the myth that classrooms should be impersonal. These teachers are also surprised when they don't have an existing relationship to fall back on with students when challenges arise. You'd be surprised how far authenticity can take you with your students.

Even the students who pretend to dislike you want to get to know you. It's usually those students who want to eat lunch with you and talk your ear off after school! When you distance yourself from your students, you actually dehumanize yourself. It's important that your kids know that you're a person with feelings, ideas, and also biases.

There are a few challenges that teachers typically face when they are trying to be authentic:

They're afraid to cross boundaries. This is especially challenging for young (or young-looking!) teachers with older students. It's very easy for kids to see you as their friend, and they'll try and bring you in! You can certainly have boundaries and still be yourself. Start by sharing one aspect of your life. Maybe you want to tell them about your experience in middle school, or maybe you have a pet to share. Start small and be intentional about what you want to share. Be open and authentic but be mindful of your boundaries. What feels right to you to share? What are you comfortable answering questions about?

They're worried about how kids will respond. This is especially true with teachers who don't share the same culture or frame of reference as their students. It is a common misconception that being culturally responsive means that you have to adopt or pretend to belong to your students' cultures. That is not the case! Of course, representation matters, and it is meaningful for students of color to see people who look like them in the classroom. But white teachers can be highly effective with students of color. I worked with a young teacher who did an emergency credentialing program. She was from rural Minnesota and was placed in Plaquemine, Louisiana. When we talked about being ourselves in front of the kids, she said she was embarrassed to tell them she was a Swiftie (Taylor Swift superfan) and grew up snowboarding. "I'm just so white!" We shared a laugh and I validated her concerns. Address the elephant in the room if you don't share a culture with your students. You don't have to try and fake it to connect with them; in fact, that's the opposite of what to do. Be open and honest about your likes. Kids enjoy learning about different cultures and experiences.

They're afraid kids won't take them seriously. This is a bit of a mindset shift. Many teachers think that they can only have control over their classrooms if they have an authoritarian presence. You absolutely want a sense of authority in the classroom; it's ultimately your responsibility to keep kids safe and lead the community in the right direction. But you don't have to be a looming authority figure to accomplish this. Kids seeing you as a human won't damage your position in the classroom. In fact, it might help the students feel more connected with you. Kids respond better to people with whom they have a relationship. They can't have a relationship with you if they don't know you.

Single-Subject Teachers and elective Teachers

When you work with all the kids in the school it can seem daunting to try and build a relationship with every single one. It should certainly be your goal to have rapport with each student and know their families if you can, but don't overwhelm yourself or feel guilty if you can't manage to be everyone's favorite teacher.

In the best-case scenario, you'll have a strong alliance with other teachers and classroom teachers if you are an elective or specials teacher. The classroom teacher can provide you with plenty of opportunities to spend time with the students and build connections.

If you're a specials teacher at a school with single-subject teachers, you generally have two approaches: you can learn the practices of the classroom teachers and mimic their ecosystem. Alternatively, you can have students develop a different ecosystem when they're in your room.

If you use the systems that are already being employed in their classrooms, then students have one less thing to learn and juggle. If you make your own systems, then students will have something else to juggle, but you can create a unique and distinct culture in the classroom.

Whatever direction you choose, a common mistake that all teachers make is to rush into content. It can seem silly to spend 10 out of your 30 minutes a week on culture, but it ends up paying off in the long term.

Middle school teachers have similar challenges. Some have over a 100 students, and it's daunting to think that you can build relationships with all of them in a timely fashion. You absolutely can get there, and it'll start with small things, like learning their names and greeting them at the door.

Building relationships in middle school can be challenging, but it's these students who need their teachers the most. The loss of a dedicated classroom teacher can be challenging for some students. Middle school teachers should use their classroom time early in the year to find time to connect with students. There are also many options to bring identity work and relationship building into an academic context as well.

You have to learn how to walk a fine line. You don't want your students to live in fear of you, but you want them to respect you.

BUILDING RELATIONSHIPS

Between constant testing, observations, and scope-and-sequence fatigue, it can seem challenging to fit in relationship building. Still, this is a shift we must make. The relationships are the glue, the web that holds your ecosystem together, and they have to be the priority.

Sometimes I meet frustrated teachers who feel pressure to rush into content or push forward with a lesson instead of taking the time to build relationships. I get it—there's a looming clock or deadline ticking away with standards to be addressed. So they jump in, thinking that they don't have time.

Fast forward to November, when the 60 instructional minutes are looking more like 120 because it just takes so long to get through the material.

You're doing your direct instruction and you have to redirect students four or five times. Then you give your small-group instructions, but once they're in breakout groups you spend more time putting out fires than differentiating. So maybe you start spending less times in independent work and groups, because management is difficult. But your students struggle just as much trying to sit through direct instruction for too long. So then you think, maybe we should do more group or independent work. You're in this cycle, over and over. So did you really save that time? Or did it just get broken up into five minutes here and five minutes there that you lost of instructional time? Investing time in relationships will always pay off in the classroom. Remember, you cannot love your kids if you don't know them.

There isn't a hierarchy in the ecosystem, and the teacher should not consider themselves as the center. But it is critical that the teacher fosters positive relationships with each and every student. To again quote the late great Rita Pierson, you don't have to like each and every student, but they aren't going to learn from someone whom they think doesn't like them.

There's an overall classroom culture, and at the same time, there's also a need for individual relationships. It's critical that the teacher builds relationships with the students, but it's also crucial that the students have positive relationships with each other. Your ecosystem won't thrive if the students don't feel a collective sense of community. That sense of belonging doesn't just come from the teacher; the students have to see themselves and where they fit within the larger student community as well. When something goes wrong or harm is done, part of the response is to help the student understand why their actions negatively affected the community. If the students don't have empathy for each other and have personal relationships with each other, they won't care about affecting the community.

Relationship building is done in 1,000 little ways (Figure 4.1). For some teachers, they naturally feel comfortable, others need more intention and structure to make sure it actually gets done. If relationship building doesn't come naturally to you, you might need to consider operationalizing it in some way. We will talk more about specific relationship-building tactics and practices in Chapter 5.

Again, is it your job to build relationships? I think so. Think about it this way. If you go to your job description, it might not say "build relationships with students." Most job descriptions include covering the material in the curriculum and it'll likely say something about keeping kids safe. Can you do those things if you have no relationship with your students?

Think about your favorite teacher or a teacher whom you thought was particularly effective. You probably had some kind of relationship with them. Think about someone whom you learned a lot from. Maybe it was coach, grandparent, even a mentor. You likely had a relationship with that person. There was something that made them have an impact on you, something more than just really good pedagogy.

Most teachers understand that relationships are important, but some just don't feel that there is space to cultivate these relationships. Concerns about teacher's bandwidth and workload are valid. Teachers can't do everything. But when it's time to decide what to prioritize, relationships

Figure 4.1 Essential Elements of Teacher-Student Relationships

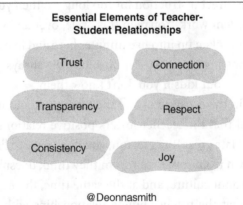

@Deonnasmith

should be close to the top of the list. When strong relationships are in place, everything flows more smoothly. In fact, students who have positive relationships with their teachers are less likely to be chronically absent, have better social emotional skills, have higher intrinsic motivation, and, overall, higher academic performance in school (Coristine et al., 2022).

Remember, relationships are not just the means through which you can get your students to have more academic success. They are also an outcome within themselves. Grade-level standards are focused on academics, but as teachers, we know that there is much more to the classroom. We want our students to walk away knowing the standards concerning literacy and numeracy, but we also know the long lasting impact of healthy connections and relationships.

Building relationships with your students will not make all of the institutional barriers to their success go away. Building relationships is not a substitute for mental health resources and support. But building relationships will absolutely help the classroom ecosystem flourish!

Sometimes when we talk about schooling and teaching, we create two distinct silos: teaching and instruction and culture and community. This is a false dichotomy and only adds to teacher workload. When you separate community building from instruction it becomes an either/or not a both/and. Building relationships and creating a healthy classroom ecosystem becomes one more thing to do.

Instead, focus on how these two ideas intertwine and reinforce each other. If you have strong instructional practices, students will be more engaged, more excited about learning, and more motivated to be a part of the classroom ecosystem. It's the same with relationships. If kids have healthy relationships with their teachers, they're more invested in learning and they are actually in a place to participate in instruction. Some students are experiencing too much internally and emotionally, whether it be stress, trauma, fear, or any other emotion. Many students don't have the tools to grapple with these emotions, so they divest away from learning time. When they have solid relationships with their teachers, they can be drawn back in.

Building relationships and building high-quality instructional practices can be interdependent. In every lesson there is space to make your students feel seen, loved, or connect with them. When we reject the dichotomy and either/or thinking, and instead see these classroom culture and instruction as connected, we can strategize about practices that support both strong instructional practices and a healthy community, instead of trying to juggle both.

Classrooms with Other Supporting Adults

But what about your students who have another trusted adult in the classroom? Para-professionals, behavior interventionists, and classroom aides all can make or break your year. In an ideal world, all teachers would have some kind of help and support in the classroom. That is not the reality for most teachers, but some students will have a dedicated support adult because of their IEP or other needs.

This is a positive thing; there is no such thing as a student having too many healthy relationships with adults. But it's worth noting that students who have a one-on-one support person may not have a close relationship with their teachers. If you experience this, it's important that you don't see this as an out.

I worked with a very large school in Arizona that had a student who was diagnosed as oppositional defiant, or having ODD. The young lady, Jade, had quite a reputation around the school. Many teachers would compare battle scars after having Jade in their class. As Jade got older and her episodes became more explosive, she was eventually assigned a one-on-one before going into the 5th grade. The 5th grade teacher was ecstatic: "I'm just glad I don't have to deal with her!" Her aide was with her for the entire school day except for recess, when Jade didn't typically have challenges. The teacher didn't give work or assignments to the student; everything went through the aide. It was the aide who called home when there was a problem, who helped de-escalate Jade, and who listened to the updates about what was going on in her life.

Everything was fine until the aide needed more flexibility in her schedule because she was pregnant. Jade's teacher was so terrified that she would have an outburst that she didn't see the opportunity to build the relationship. If Jade's teacher had made some effort early to build a substantive relationship with Jade, when the aide left, she wouldn't have to start from the ground up.

Students with IEPs or who have big behavior issues are entitled to extra support, but that doesn't mean that they don't also need a functional and dependable relationship with their teacher. Ideally, the teacher should have a strong understanding and familiarity with the needs of the student anyway. This is not at all to diminish the incredible work that para-professionals do, but at the end of the day, the student is still in the teacher's class with the rest of the community. They still need to feel like they are part of the ecosystem. Teachers in this position should take extra time to ensure that they are still connecting with the student and the support team. When the support team, family, and teacher are all on the same page, the student can truly thrive.

CREATING AN INTERDEPENDENT ECOSYSTEM

The next step is to start to reimagine and build your ecosystem. What tools and strategies will you use to ensure it is healthy?

You'll have to think through all of the important proactive measures, such as establishing norms, hosting morning meetings, and building relationships. At the same time acknowledge the reality that you'll need a plan for when things steer off course. You'll want to think through what makes sense for your school, but also what makes sense for you. For example, if you're already overwhelmed, a complicated system with different coupons and trinkets might not be for you.

Here's some questions to consider as you get started:

- What is my plan for building relationships with students?
- What is my strategy to engage families as stakeholders?
- How will I support students in making the small, good decisions, such as raising their hand and staying on task?
- How will I respond when students don't make good decisions?
- What strategies will I use to de-escalate students when they're having big emotions?
- How will I bring joy into the classroom each and every day?
- How do I need to invest in myself so that I have the bandwidth to give each student a fresh start every day?

When it comes to the classroom ecosystem, remember that the systems individually are greater than sum of their parts. That is to say, each element of your ecosystem taken independently may not seem like a revolutionary and transformative practice, but when they work together, your ecosystem will thrive.

Many teachers who are frustrated by classroom management might decide to switch their practices or tactics. There are no shortage of gimmicks, games, and systems that teachers employ to manage their classrooms. Some teachers have great success with classroom economy, Class Dojo, or treasure boxes; for others, each of those systems falls flat.

Although there are a million reasons why a system might not work, consider this: if we think about our classroom as an ecosystem, we can understand that the systems are interdependent on each other. You might give out points, but if students don't understand empathy then they'll start behaving only to receive points instead of to be kind to each other.

You might ask students who are misbehaving to leave the classroom. Many teachers when they are frustrated send kids to the office or even to a buddy classroom. But one of the most frequent antecedents for students acting out is work avoidance. The more time they spend outside of the classroom, the more they'll fall behind.

One system or one strategy is often not enough. For your ecosystem to be healthy you might need a few different strategies that are interdependent on each other. I was working with a school in Florida that was experiencing severe behavior challenges and issues. The principal decided to implement a new system to support the lower elementary teachers. Clip charts were rolled out as a requirement for K–3. Now, clip charts are already a controversial management strategy. There's quite a bit of research that suggests that public displays do more harm than good and the clip moving up and down can be very punitive (King, 2022). Kids aren't really internalizing a consequence of their action or understanding that their behaviors can cause harm, instead they hyper-focus on an external metric like a clip. But the school was getting desperate and went ahead with the strategy, and saw little success for two reasons. First, purely external motivators like clip charts are often ineffective for the highest-need students. Your students who are eager to please might be even more compliant, and there are a few kids in every class who'll go along with any system regardless.

The second reason is that in this school struggle the clip charts weren't really part of a larger vision, goal, or ecosystem. They wanted to reinforce specific behaviors such as kindness and address what many schools would call tier 1 behaviors such as talking out of turn or not being in your seat. But the school didn't couple the clip chart with any community builders, procedure reenforcement, or reflection time to notice the antecedents of the behavior.

But what if you're required to work within the confines of a school-wide system? The classroom ecosystem can still flourish! Depending on how much flexibility you have within the school-wide system, you may be able to make small adjustments to the school-wide plan in a way that suits your ecosystem. For example, I worked at a school that required the use of Class Dojo, but the points system felt too punitive. Instead of taking away points I still used Class Dojo, but I only added points and had students work toward accruing as many as they could.

Keeping your ecosystem in balance will require both proactive and reactive work. Remember, it's just as important to cultivate positive interactions in the classroom as it is to respond to negative ones. If you only have a plan for when things go wrong, you won't be feeding the positivity and creating opportunities for joy. This is a common challenge, especially for teachers who have multiple classes or older kids. They have rules and expectations and plans for when things go wrong, but there's nothing to cultivate the positivity in the community.

Conversely some teachers don't struggle with relationship building at all. They have all the activities, protocols, and experiences and kids are joyful. But they don't have a planned response for when students act out, and then in the moment they end up jumping to something negative.

You need both for a healthy ecosystem. Sometimes teachers are more comfortable with one or the other and that's okay! The self-awareness of your strengths and weaknesses will help build an even stronger system.

Figure 4.2 outlines the key components and elements to consider of the classroom ecosystem.

It's critical to start with vision setting and freedom dreaming what the classroom ecosystem will look like and feel like. This should include your students as well! If we are willing to listen, kids will give us a wealth of information about what type of ecosystem they'd like to learn in.

One you've thought through that you can consider how to use the classroom space to work with your students and your system. The space can do quite a bit of the heavy lifting for you.

Figure 4.2 The Key Components of Classroom Ecosystems

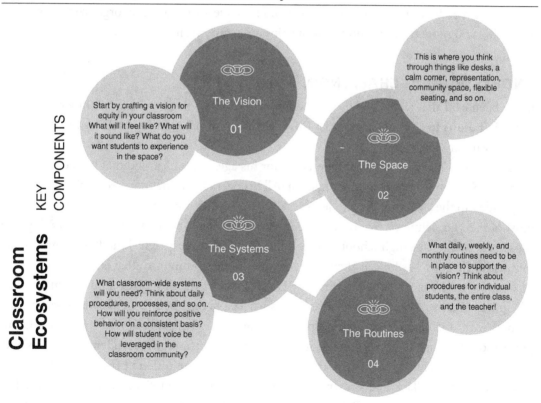

When kids feel physically comfortable and safe, they are less likely to experience the emotional distress that can often precipitate big behaviors.

The systems and routines are essential. You must think about the daily processes that will uphold your ecosystem. The day-to-day is the most tangible and critical reality for teachers. Thoughtful routines and systems that your students help cocreate can go far as proactive measures. The routine also creates a sense of security and dependability for your students. Routines and predictability also help students feel safe.

This is not to suggest that the solution is "teachers just need to do more." When you start to map out and cultivate your ecosystem, you might find yourself thinking that it all seems like a lot, or just another thing on teacher's plates. So, let's be honest, initially, it'll probably feel like more work. It takes more to get an unhealthy ecosystem back on track than to start fresh. Even when you are starting with a clean slate it's still challenging because there is so much prep work that goes in to setting up your ecosystem. In those moments, remember, the great thing about ecosystems is they are mostly self-sustaining. Once you get the classroom going and your strategies rolling, you'll notice that you have to spend much less time leading, organizing, counting, and doing and more time building relationships and empowering students!

UNDERSTANDING CHALLENGING STUDENTS

It has been said that a child who is not embraced by the village will burn it down to feel its warmth. I didn't fully understand what this meant until I met Jeremey, and boy did he try and burn down our village.

Jeremey was an 8th grader but he was big for his age. Later I learned that he seemed bigger because he'd been held back in kindergarten. All his peers knew that he'd been held back, which only added to the alienation he felt. Jeremey's school was the kind of place that kids went to for most of their academic career. They came in all together in kindergarten and left in 8th grade. Most went to the same high school and their families were all very tight-knit. It was a great community for the kids—as long as they were included in the community, that is.

Jeremey wasn't part of the community. He was one of the few Black students in an overwhelmingly Latinx school. Because I've always worked in big cities in California, I was used to schools with this demographic makeup. Most schools in California have a significant Latinx population, and then there are other groups mixed in, sometimes white students, Pacific Islanders, or Black students. Schools that are diverse in this way are different from schools that are mostly white with Black and Brown kids mixed in. Sometimes folks incorrectly assume that because all of the students are Brown or BIPOC that there is less racial tension. Unfortunately that is not always the case. People of color are navigating the same racial tensions and stereo-types as everyone else. Anti-Blackness is pervasive in many communities, including communities of color, and xenophobia is a problem in the Black community as well. Black and Brown students have to navigate racial tensions and racism in their interactions with white-dominant spaces and spaces with each other.

Middle school exacerbates these dynamics and challenges. Teenagers and preteens are trying to negotiate and understand the world around them. This is also when most identity development begins and is solidified, so it makes sense that race and ethnic identity are concerns for them. Adolescence is difficult anyway, but you add the layer of social media and our kids can really struggle!

Despite being in a cohort right along with the other kids since kindergarten, Jeremey didn't fit in anywhere. He was tall, dark-skinned, and awkward. Like all middle schoolers, he had friendships that came and went. Sometimes he'd click with a group and find some stability; other times he'd be a loner.

It was clear that the school hadn't addressed the racial tensions head on. Sometimes the kids would exchange slurs. They'd call each other terrible and offensive names and claim that it's okay because it's a "joke." They'd learn new songs and phrases in social media and promptly test them out during recess time. Most of the staff members were all white and didn't quite know how to address these issues. Some didn't want to say the wrong thing or didn't know what their place in these conversations were because they were white. Their inaction and trepidation, although understandable, was harming Jeremey.

Jeremey had always had behavior problems, but they really reached a crescendo in 8th grade. He came to most classes late, never wore the uniform, and was flagrantly disrespectful toward teachers. We're not talking about just talking out of turn or other minimally disruptive behaviors; we're talking about hateful, inappropriate, sexist, and racist comments toward the teachers and staff members. It's hard to lead with patience and understanding when you feel like you're being verbally abused by a student.

Jeremey's behavior started to strain the entire faculty. The other students were becoming openly hostile toward him. They'd taunt him in class, trip him intentionally, and isolate him during lunch and recess. On the one hand, we wanted all of our students to be inclusive; on the other hand, when Jeremey was included he treated them terribly.

We tried everything: circles, suspensions, Saturday school, detention, calling home. We got so desperate we were offering Amazon gift cards for good days. (I'm ashamed to admit it got that bad.)

What I had to do was step back and realize that I was being far too reactive. I was waiting for Jeremey to show these behaviors, then I scrambled to respond. Instead, I needed to be thinking about what was behind these behaviors. I looked for the antecedents. The first thing I noticed was that Jeremey didn't like being put on the spot and being in small groups. That was an antecedent I couldn't quite remove; I couldn't tell teachers never to call on him or never put him in groups.

I needed to look even deeper into the entire school community and how it supported (and didn't support) Jeremey. My first step was to spend a day observing. I followed him around to all the classes and tried to really see things from his point of view. I definitely saw how bad his behavior had gotten—but at the end of the day, I also saw a kid that just didn't belong.

Because the school had a strong Latinx presence in the student body and it was in a very diverse part of town, they did a pretty good job of making space for Latinx heritage and culture in the school. But there were only a handful of Black students, so there wasn't the same vibrance for Black culture. On a cultural level Jeremey wasn't visible.

The school was very much aware of the murmurs and daily challenges that Jeremey experienced due to his race, but they had been playing whack-a-mole with their responses. There wasn't a concrete, proactive plan. Instead they would take away recess or penalize the students in some way when something happened.

The truth is, the school wasn't a good place to be Black. It wasn't an environment where Blackness was celebrated. So years of internalized racism, colorism, and bullying had culminated in one angry, alienated 8th grader.

What made it more complicated was the teachers were so frustrated for so long that at that point they wanted a quick solution—but let me tell you: repairing communities takes time. We had to systemically take on anti-Blackness and start to rebuild a community that was truly inclusive.

We had to start by educating our students. We added lessons and discussions about anti-Blackness and colorism within the Latinx community into our homerooms. Students read articles, watched videos, and had roundtable discussions. We had a specific assembly to talk about racial slurs and problematic language. We doubled down on community builders, and teachers spent extra time ensuring that each student was actively participating. We invited our small but mighty group of Black families to host a lunch for some of our students. All of these things along with extra therapy for Jeremey, an adult mentor, and weekly check-ins with his family so they stayed in the loop.

It wasn't just the kids; the teachers attended two trainings as well. One on talking about issues of race in class and how to address slurs. Another session was on inclusion and anti-Blackness. The teachers needed the skill development to be able to meet their students' needs.

It would have been much easier to expel Jeremey. We could have waited it out like some teachers suggested since he was already an 8th grader. But we had such a unique opportunity to transform a student's experience. Anti-racism is also about what you do in those difficult moments. Anti-racism has to inform your decision-making in those tough moments, instead of just taking the easy way out.

It was about a mindset shift, instead of just thinking of ways to respond to Jeremey's behavior. We had to think about the harm that had been caused within our community and how to heal from it. The results were not perfect. There were certainly fewer bad days, but that doesn't mean that Jeremey's behavior was always wonderful. What was perhaps most important was that the students began to think critically about what it meant to be in community with each other and build relationships grounded in anti-racism.

We focus quite a bit on building relationships when we think about how to have a healthy classroom culture, but the relationships between the students have to be strong and healthy. They are the webs that hold the ecosystem together.

I've seen quite a few schools that have an overall strong school culture, but they have a few students that don't fit in or struggle with extreme behaviors. Because kids are kids and they don't always communicate their needs in an appropriate way, that's why we see so many attention seeking behaviors. Sometimes, these students with big behaviors can get stuck in a feedback loop.

They have big behaviors that clearly disrupt or disturb the class. The other students see these behaviors. At first the other students might ignore or even hype up the negative behaviors. Eventually the other students might get tired and frustrated of behaviors, and so will the teacher. The student becomes more isolated and more of a pariah, which makes them act out even more!

It's difficult to break this cycle because for so many children any attention is better than none at all. When you're thinking about how to respond to these behaviors, you can't just address the student; you need to ensure that you're finding a place for them in the community. The other students might be grappling with their own frustrations or resentments toward that student that they themselves have to heal. In these situations, invest the time in circles and community-building opportunities. The students will be looking to the teacher and taking notes from them about how to interact with students with behavior challenges. If you act like you're harboring resentment and anger toward a student because of their past behaviors, the kids will, too.

Sometimes teachers start to over-empathize with the students who are excluded, because they share the same frustration. It is absolutely true that we need to see both sides. If I were a student who was focused and a kind and helpful community member each day, I would be extremely frustrated by a student who was continuously harming the classroom community. But for a struggling student to be included, the parties that were harmed, in this case the other students and the teacher, have to move forward from the previous challenges and welcome the student back into the community with a clean slate.

If you're troubleshooting a behavior response and you've found strategies that work for your challenging students, but you aren't seeing a shift, you'll want to turn your attention to making sure that the rest of the classroom ecosystem has found a way to heal and move forward.

FAMILIES AND COMMUNITIES

The classroom ecosystem is much more than just you and your students. Their families need space as well. Too often teachers only think about engaging families. What does it mean to engage? This looks like sending letters home, communicating, and finding opportunities for them to participate in the community. But engaging isn't enough.

Historically, schools have been used to divorce students from their home and native cultures. Families were shut out of schools as a way to ensure that schools were able to indoctrinate students into white American values (Center on Education Policy, 2020). Our schools are still grappling with that today.

Most schools want families to engage and participate, but only on the school's terms. Families don't necessarily share decision-making power, and they aren't viewed as equal stakeholders. Instead they are informed about what is being implemented and offered very controlled opportunities to be a part of the school community.

For your practices to be rooted in equity, you must push back against frameworks that value the dominant culture over students' native cultures.

We want to engage families in authentic ways, but we also need to recognize their strengths, expertise, and inherent value. You'll want a mix of the following activities and tools:

Ways to Bring Families In
- Back to school night, family math night, family days, and so on
- Newsletters/updates
- Family communication management system such SchoolReach or Parent Square
- Conferences
- Celebrations for heritage months
- Funraisers and fundraisers
- Workshops
- Family book clubs
- Room parents or other programs for volunteers

Ways for Families to Be Stakeholders

- PTA or some kind of family advisory body
- Decision-making on curriculum
- Participation in the hiring process

Note that this should not be conflated with the surge of anti-CRT and frankly racist rhetoric in the wake of the social uprisings of 2020. Across the nation, angry families at school board meetings are fighting to have more control over what is taught inside the classroom. These sentiments are not rooted in experience, research, or even facts. Families should be part of the school community, but it is not the job of an individual teacher to respond to and navigate this impact of this troubling trend alone. School leaders and policy makers must support teachers as well.

Here are some additional considerations.

What could it look like at your school for families to be stakeholders in decision-making?

Teachers must find ways to build relationships with their communities. Again we have to look at the legacy of the public school system. Schools have been used intentionally to sever the ties that students have with their communities. This still happens, especially when a public school becomes a charter or a turnaround. When these organizations come in, they can make the strategic and well-informed choice to maintain ties and respect with the existing community. Or they can come in and operate the school in isolation.

In *We Want to Do More Than Survive* Bettina Love freedom dreams community schools, places where the schools exist as an integral part of the community and respond to its needs. The schools bolster the community and foster pride for the students, as opposed to schools that perpetuate brain drain in communities (Love, 2019). *Brain drain* refers to when members of the community participate in formalized structures of education and leave their communities, exporting all the investment from the students' home into a different community.

What can teachers do to build community schools?

A school that I worked with in Los Angeles did an excellent job of integrating itself into the community. New staff members did a community scavenger hunt, where they experienced the world that their students live in. They took the route that many students followed to get to school and soaked up all that it meant to be part of the neighborhood.

The school also had a dedicated staff member who worked to build community with families and other local organizations. If a family had a question about immigration, legal services, housing assistance, or health care, there were trained folks on staff who knew how to help.

Local community-based organizations partnered with the school often to provide services and share information. For the families, the school was a community hub. Kids were proud to be part of the community and the community was proud of the school.

How does all this tie into behavior?

It all comes back to culture and belonging. When students see and feel that their school values them as they are, and their culture, they are able to be the fullest versions of themselves at school. When schools isolate other students' cultures it creates an additional barrier for students to have to overcome to be successful at school.

It's also helpful for teachers to build their context and frame of reference. The more you understand about your students and their lives, the easier it will be for you to build relationships with them. The best way to start? Be curious! Be curious about where your kids live, where they come from, and their stories.

THE SECRET INGREDIENT IS *JOY*

At the root of your community must be joy. Joy has the ability to liberate student potential and build relationships. When I scroll through my social media comments, every once in a while I'll see some from my students. They leave me nice comments and ask for updates on how I'm doing. I try to stay in contact with my kids and their families as much as possible. I believe deeply that because we are sowing seeds, it may take a while to see the flowers that bloom. By keeping up with my kids, I'm able to see the big picture, not just what they were like in my classroom. When I talk to them, my students remember the most peculiar things about our class. It never ceases to amaze me the small little details that they are able to bring to mind.

They don't typically remember the exact things that I teach them. Of course at some level they remember what we went over, because the ideas and lessons build and they continue to become more and more critical thinkers and problem-solvers. But unless there's a big "a-ha" moment, they don't typically remember learning anything specific. What they always remember is how they felt in my class and the joyful times that we had together.

I circled back with a student not too long ago and she was explaining to her friends that I used to be her favorite teacher. I thought she'd say something about us both being Black women or about us both loving math and Beyonce, but what she remembered most was a field trip to a museum. Museum field trips are hit or miss, and this one was pretty miss. The kids didn't really read the descriptions and were basically just meandering around while I told them to lower their voices every six to nine minutes. By the end I was frustrated. I wanted my kids, who didn't typically do these kinds of things on the weekend, to have a diverse roster of experiences to draw from. I felt like they threw it back in my face by being woefully uninterested in everything our docent had to say. I was feeling pretty irritated and frustrated with them. We were on our way back to the bus after the museum and I remembered that it was Free Cone Day at Ben and Jerry's. For a second, I thought, do they really deserve ice cream? They didn't really "earn" it. At that time having good control and management over my kids was a huge point of pride for me. I have to admit I felt embarrassed in the museum. My kids who were usually the shining example were not their best selves at the museum.

To be honest, at the end of the day, my own love of Phish Food got the best of me. There just happened to be a Ben and Jerry's about a quarter mile away. I made a split-second decision, told the bus we'd be late, and walked all my kids to Free Cone Day. Have you ever told a bunch of 10-year-olds that they're getting free surprise ice cream during the school day? We sang songs on the way and rolled up to Ben and Jerry's in one excited and chaotic blob. We laughed and sang in the line, told stories over ice cream, and made sure to tip the servers generously. It ended up being one of the best days that I ever spent with that class—and this student remembered it. I almost missed it, this opportunity to give some kids the "best day ever" for free. All because I was feeling embarrassed about my own management.

As I learned more about the world, injustice, and teaching I realized that joy absolutely had to be at the center of my classroom. The world is a rough place for both kids and adults, but for my Black and Brown kids especially. There are so many teachers who don't have the capacity and bandwidth to know better and do better. So they stick to antiquated ideas about what a classroom should be. But think about what we are all going through: mass shootings, climate change, racism, the fallout of COVID-19. Did they really need yet another person who was rationing their joy? Our kids need a break sometimes. We need a break sometimes.

It's not always that simple, even if it should be. A challenge that many teachers face is how to let students start to explore, have more agency, and find those moments, while still making sure the classroom is safe.

When I was coaching teachers I worked with Ms. Benning. Ms. Benning had what I lovingly refer to as summer camp energy. Summer camp leaders and teachers are some of the most important adults in a kids life. They make great connections with students and the concept of making things joyful comes very easily to them. In these environments the expectations of kids are a little different and they don't have the same looming pressure of observations and standards. Depending on the structure of their program, afterschool teachers might have this energy as well. I believe that daytime teachers can learn a lot from these types of teachers but the jobs are not the same. When a teacher comes from a summer camp or afterschool background, the joyful aspect of teaching comes naturally, but they may sometimes struggle with balancing that with the academic demands and the reality of keeping kids safe.

Kids can absolutely be joyful and safe! But it's not as easy as saying let's be more joyful! Ms. Benning tried to find ways to bring joy into her classroom. She had had a very rough start to her year. She didn't quite have that "teacher voice" and she looked very young. The kids, quite plainly, didn't take her seriously and she was working with a fairly challenging cohort of middle schoolers. The week before I had given a PD on incorporating joy. Ms. Benning was excited about the PD and asked me to come observe her the following week. She had a set of standards that she was wrapping up and instead of doing a basic review she decided to do a Kahoot, inspired by our joy conversation. Before I was even in the classroom I was nervous for her. This was their first Kahoot, it was Friday, she was giving out candy as a prize, the students could pick their own teams, and it was the period right after lunch.

Again, assume best intentions, be asset based, but my gut was telling me that this might be a challenge for her. I observed the lesson and—what I saw was a teacher that truly found joy in building relationships with her students. She had gone to a high-resource "hippie" school—her words—where teachers were called by their first names and kids filled out their own report cards. I thought the school sounded great, but that wasn't our school.

She had put so much time into creating questions. She had a little microphone and props. I could tell that there was so much care and attention to detail put into creating that lesson. But when it was time to play, all hell broke loose.

The students were shouting, shoving, giving their teams inappropriate names, calling out the answers; it was just chaotic. I was feeling dysregulated after just 10 minutes so I knew everyone else was feeling it, too! When a student fell out of his chair and hit his head on the textbook rack, it was time to call it. We stopped the Kahoot and pivoted to a few minutes of quiet mindfulness.

Afterward Ms. Benning was understandably very upset. "This is why we can't do anything fun! They ruin it! I don't want to be boring and hardcore but they gave me no choice!"

I felt for her, she put in a lot of time and it did not yield the results that she was looking for. After some space to vent and shed a few tears, we were ready to talk about what happened and what she would do differently.

She told me that what she'd do differently would be to not have done the game at all. I know she was frustrated, but I shared with her that this was not actually the solution. This is where so many teachers find themselves. Frustrated by behavior and feeling like they have no leeway to do anything fun.

I asked her, at the end the day did she believe that her kids deserved to have a review day that wasn't just direct instruction? She did. I asked if she thought that her kids *could* participate in a Kahoot? She wasn't sure if they had the capacity to do it safely. I disagreed.

I disagree fundamentally with the idea that some kids just don't have the capacity and ability to do developmentally appropriate things safely. Will some need more prep? Yes, but thinking that some kids just can't have fun at school is not using an asset-based approach.

Ms. Benning isn't the only teacher who felt this way. I've worked with many teachers who feel like they can't let go of control in their classrooms because it will descend into chaos. When teachers feel like they can't manage a classroom, then they revert back to stricter and less joyful methods. It comes from a good place, a genuine concern for safety. But ecosystems that don't have space for joy just can't thrive.

I frequently talk to teacher who say their kids can't do group work or talk while they're working because they can't do it quietly. It is difficult for me to believe that there exists a classroom where kids have to be regulated to carceral practices because they can't learn how to work collaboratively. Maybe they can't go from silent rows to picking their own partners right away, but they can get there.

Back to Ms. Benning, I started to ask her about the preparations. Had they done Kahoots before? Were the expectations clear? Did they have a chance to practice playing before it was go time? Did they all put themselves in situations and groups that made sense? What steps did you take to make sure everyone understood why safety would be important? And what might happen if someone wasn't safe?

Ms. Benning had spent so much time prepping for the game that she wasn't thinking about setting the students up for success. Here's the thing: you shouldn't ration joy in the classroom, but you absolutely need to launch it.

Consider a few things:

- Students might not be used to being able to be uninhibited, so when they can be they go all out.
- Students might not have a frame of reference or experience with certain games and activities, so they won't automatically know how to do them safely.
- Kids have more fun when they understand boundaries because everyone can participate appropriately.
- Once students practice and get the routines down, they'll have even more fun.

Decentralizing the classroom and finding more space for joy is like instruction: it requires preparation, chunking, and intention, but it also becomes second nature.

I asked Ms. Benning what she would do differently if she absolutely had to do the same activity. After some reflection she mentioned that she should have realized that the kids needed to be scaffolded with the rollout of the Kahoot. We talked about a lot of ideas, but here are a few. It really all boils down to setting them up for success.

- She could have had a small community meeting to plan with students for how they'd play the Kahoot safely.
- The kids could work up to selecting their own teams and start with their table partners at the beginning.
- They could try a shorter, lower-stakes Kahoot to practice.
- She could review the classroom norms before getting started.
- Even if things didn't go well, she could have held a circle with students to give them a chance to reflect on how they might do better in the future.

Joy should never be something that you withhold or dangle over students. When I walk in to classrooms that have major challenges, ones where the ecosystem has become dysfunctional and the teacher thinks about running out the door *every day*, I'll often start with joy. Sometimes people are shocked. They're expecting a turnaround. We start with small, community experiences that bring students together, instead of cracking down with harsh or reactionary procedures. Some teachers think that it's not important because the students are already running the classroom and might seem like they're having fun in class. But when you take a step back, these ecosystems are usually not joyful. Even if a classroom is dysfunctional and students aren't actually getting any work done, that doesn't mean that they feel like they belong, cared for, and joyful.

JOY IN EQUITY WORK

When people think about abolition, anti-racism, and other equity work they think it's all about struggle. Maybe it's because we use words like *fight* and *dismantle*. Words that sound like we are going to war. And in some ways, that's true. We absolutely must battle systems of oppression in education, but that doesn't mean that it's all about labor, work, and strife.

Quite the opposite.

What our kids need, especially our Black and Brown babies, is a safe space to be joyful. Joy in and of itself is resistance. When we prioritize joy, we refuse to let these systems rob us of the complexity of our humanity. We push back against the idea that school is where kids need to be controlled. We don't fear noise, enthusiasm, messiness, and the energy that joy can bring into our classroom. We welcome it with open arms and celebrate the fact that our kids have a space to unabashedly feel and cultivate joy.

This book doesn't label joy as a strategy. It's not just a means to get kids to learn more. Joy is the goal. It is not an add-on, but rather a fundamental belief and value. Joy is at the root of your ecosystem. It is the seed from which the rest of your ecosystem grows. Start with joy, and watch as your ecosystem flourishes.

Maintaining the Ecosystem

M ost healthy ecosystems are self-sufficient. The different organisms interact with each other in balanced and appropriate ways. If you're a teacher, when you think about the classroom ecosystem, ideally things will start to run themselves. But that doesn't mean that you can just step back and watch; maintaining a classroom takes work!

Maintaining a classroom ecosystem is different than traditional classroom-management strategies in two ways. First, in the classroom ecosystem rooted in joy, the teacher plays a primarily proactive role, not a reactive one. Not the person who polices students, waiting for them to not meet expectations, or punishing them when they don't follow the rules. Instead, position yourself as the person who is working to ensure that students feel joyful, included, and safe.

Second, you are thinking holistically—not just considering individual behaviors. For the classroom to be rooted in joy, you have to be able to recognize the barriers that might be getting in the way. Look for the roots. Practice seeing your students in their full humanity, and remind yourself that they're navigating challenges on multiple levels. At a minimum, they're growing up, maturing, figuring out their identities. They're learning how to juggle the ups and downs of family and friends. (And we can't forget how, on top of all this, some of students are also facing systemic and institutional oppression.)

Following are some guiding practices to help you maintain the classroom ecosystem. First are items you'll want to consider in advance to set the stage for students' success. Following those are the items to guide you in the classroom. The last group offers guidelines to turn to as needed. But first, a reminder that it all starts with you!

STARTING WITH YOU

We already talked about all the deep and internal work that teachers need to do to unpack personal biases. But there's a reason why behavior can be such a tense subject. Student behaviors can trigger our own emotions and frustrations. It's absolutely normal to have a response to students, but it's critical that teachers are mindful of what they're bringing to every interaction. Ideally, each day—even each hour—is a fresh start. Our kids can go from having a terrible morning to an amazing afternoon. And although it makes sense to ensure that there are consequences for kids' behaviors, once the behavior has been addressed both parties have to move on. That's not always easy as a teacher, because we don't always get time to cool off or process what's happening. But prioritizing your self-care will help you navigate those tricky moments.

Remember to reference the Teacher Self Check-In framework from Chapter 1 frequently to check in with yourself.

Let's look at another example to demonstrate why it's important to check in with yourself. If I have the pleasure of working with a teacher for a day or more, I sometimes notice a pattern: a student who's been showing some harmful behaviors all day or even all week gets more closely monitored than the other students are. It makes sense because the teacher might want to anticipate challenges before they become too disruptive. But there's a flip side: if that happens, it can become an issue of confirmation bias. For example, the student exhibits a behavior, gets redirected by the teacher, and then moves on about their day—but the teacher might still be hyperaware and on edge. So, later in the afternoon, let's say the student interrupts another student, or something that is a tier 1 behavior. When the teacher responds, they're not be responding to that recent behavior—instead they're responding to the days and/or weeks leading up to that behavior.

To make matters worse I've seen teachers incredibly frustrated because teachers often call for support but support isn't always available. Or maybe they send a student out for a break, and the student was sent right back from the office. The teacher might start responding from a place of escalation. As we know, this is not the ideal state to respond to a student issue. The teacher's emotional response makes sense, but it still might not help the situation. It is of the upmost importance that teachers prioritize their own well-being and mental health so that they don't show up depleted in these situations. The more your tank is empty, the harder it is for you to show grace with your students. The worst-case scenario? You are visibly dysregulated and end up further dysregulating the student whom you're interacting with.

In these cases teachers are also in danger of reacting in a way that harms the student relationship or escalates a situation to an extreme. For example, in my early years of teaching a student wasn't following my directions. It was something simple, I wanted him come join the small group at the kidney table. I had asked a few times, and he didn't listen. We ended up going back and forth. I told him that if he didn't come to the table he'd miss recess, and then he said he didn't care, so then I said if he didn't come he'd have to stay after school. Now, I did not want to stay after school! But when you give a student an ultimatum, especially in a public space, you have to stick to it. I should have listened to my own rule about avoiding power struggles.

I was not starting with myself. I was not doing my own internal work. I was reacting to my student instead of responding to him. It starts and ends with you!

SET THE STAGE FOR SUCCESS

To truly envision and cultivate a classroom culture rooted in joy, belonging, and care, you have to examine your mindsets and beliefs about school, classrooms, and kids. Once you've engaged with that work, it's important to take the next step and align your actions with your beliefs. It's going to come down to what you do or sometimes don't do in the classroom.

Building Good Habits

"We are what we repeatedly do. Excellence, then, is not an act, but a habit."

—Aristotle

You'll want to start building some habits. This is the regularly scheduled maintenance for your ecosystem. When you're first adopting some of these habits, start slow. You might already even be doing some of these things. Maybe some won't work as they are described here in the classroom. Use these as a starting point, and remember the trick is to be consistent. Doing a few ice breakers one time or in isolation won't transform the classroom culture. But building a steady toolbox and cadence of practices will.

There are no checklists in this work, but Figure 5.1 will give you a good idea of where to start.

Figure 5.1 How to Build Community

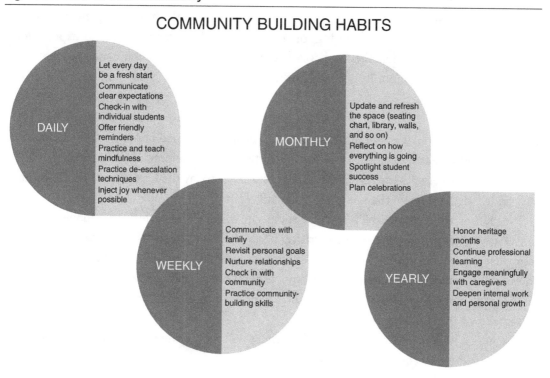

COMMUNITY BUILDING HABITS

DAILY
Let every day be a fresh start
Communicate clear expectations
Check-in with individual students
Offer friendly reminders
Practice and teach mindfulness
Practice de-escalation techniques
Inject joy whenever possible

WEEKLY
Communicate with family
Revisit personal goals
Nurture relationships
Check in with community
Practice community-building skills

MONTHLY
Update and refresh the space (seating chart, library, walls, and so on)
Reflect on how everything is going
Spotlight student success
Plan celebrations

YEARLY
Honor heritage months
Continue professional learning
Engage meaningfully with caregivers
Deepen internal work and personal growth

Edutainment, Engagement, and Investment

When you take a hard look at the antecedents for some of the behaviors in your classroom, you might notice a common thread when students are not engaged. In my experience, a strong, engaging lesson was some of the very best behavior management. But when we don't have control over our curriculum choices and the day is absolutely packed, it can be challenging to figure out how to make every second engaging—many of us are a far cry from Pinterest pages of high-energy teachers who seem to put on a show all day, every day.

Engagement can sometimes start to feel like yet another buzzword. We do want kids to be actively engaged in learning, and typically the more kids are engaged, they less likely they are to have big behaviors, but that doesn't mean that it's your job to put on a show every day. When we demand that teachers "edutain" their students we establish a pace that's unsustainable. And we have some steep competition: research has suggested that the overall attention span of students is decreasing, partially due to the oversaturation of video games and high-frames-per-minute TV shows (Bhat, 2017).

Instead of focusing on engagement, I like to talk to teachers about investment. How can we get student invested in this learning? The same goes for the classroom ecosystem. How can you get students investing in the health and well-being of the classroom community? How can they become just as invested as you are in keeping it thriving?

When the classroom culture is not the sole responsibility of the teacher, it's much easier for students to engage. They aren't waiting for the teacher to lay out the rules and expectations; instead, they build them together and collectively hold each other accountable. Students who are invested in their community show a clear indicator of a healthy ecosystem!

Procedures 101

At some point in your credentialing process you probably learned about procedures and systems. In a natural ecosystem, the elements understand how to interact with each other, but in a classroom ecosystem, it's the responsibility of the teacher to lay the foundation. This is going to vary widely depending on the age group you work with.

Procedures and routines help the classroom run smoothly and feel dependable, but they don't have to feel robotic. Messaging is critical here. Make sure students understand that they're following procedures so they can be safe and productive—not just to follow rules for the sake of rules. When students have challenges meeting expectations, it's important to not jump to compliance. You want your students' buy-in; then they need to understand *why* these procedures exist and how they help the community.

Teachers who work with our youngest learners will have quite a few procedures. Here are some critical ones to consider:

- Transitioning
- Shared supplies
- Using the restroom and communicating needs
- Personal space awareness

Some procedures for older kids could include these:

- Cell phone expectations
- Make-up work/absentee work
- Arriving on time

You'll probably see ideas all across the internet about how to establish routines for all these areas. The trick is, most will work. For example, some teachers have songs to help kids transition, some have a bell, a timer, a hand signal. Some teachers use a sign-out sheet, a pass, or just have students walk out when they want to use the bathroom. Kindergarteners and middle schoolers alike might learn about bubble space, or their personal bubble.

Every school and sometimes even each individual teacher deals with the cell phone question differently. My best advice to teachers is to find procedures and routines that work best for you and that are natural. Stick to those. Teach them directly to students at the beginning of the year and after winter break. Review them after long weekends and breaks. Procedures will be an integral component of your ecosystem. It is always worth the time and energy to ensure that all students understand them.

Whether you have older kids or younger kids it can be helpful to talk through or outline some of these procedures together. The teacher should have an idea of what it looks like, but student buy-in can be powerful.

Remember, you'll want to review these policies. The first couple days, you'll probably go over procedures for hours a day. Still, expect to do a refresh multiple times throughout the year.

You can reserve the right to switch things up. Maybe the way you thought students would pass in their papers doesn't flow like you imagined. That's okay! You can shift what's not working for you.

Hold kids accountable, but don't expect perfection. When I was a teacher I was always coached to "wait for 100%" or wait until all of my students were perfectly compliant. I think that's a great goal, but now I understand that an obsession with perfection is a vestige of white supremacy culture. So I work with my kids to strive for our best every day and keep learning.

But if I have a student who sometimes forgets to raise their hand, I don't internalize it as me being a bad teacher or them being a bad student.

The physical space can greatly help or hinder the work that you're trying to do in the classroom. Consider the classroom walk-through tool in Figure 5.2 as a starting point to building the classroom ecosystem.

Figure 5.2 My Classroom Walk-Through

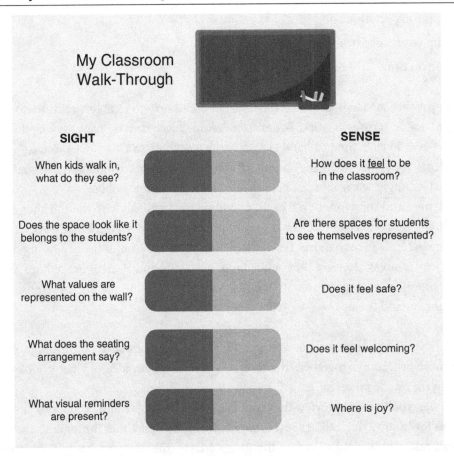

Incorporating and Layering Strategies in the Classroom Ecosystem

Many teachers work in schools where they have to use a specific system or approach, but that doesn't mean that you can't also have a joyful and inclusive classroom ecosystem. You can build a large toolbox of strategies and practices with the philosophy of joy, care, and belonging at the center. For example, some students might need incremental reinforcement or a goal to work toward. They might benefit from having a sticker chart or weekly goal-setting meetings to help support them in the classroom.

If you aren't sure if a system you already use is aligned with the overall goal of a joyful ecosystem, consider a few questions:

- Is this rule in place because it reduces harm or because it seeks to control?
- Are the consequences in fact consequences or are they punishments?
- Is the teacher's role in this system to police and monitor students or encourage and support them?
- Does the system foster community or is it centered on individualistic values?

There isn't an all-inclusive yes or no list that lays out which systems are harmful and which are not. Some systems are clearly not culturally responsive or rooted in joy—such as zero-tolerance policies—but most depend on how the teacher is using them.

When you start layering your strategies, consider both proactive community-building measures and reactive strategies to respond to student behaviors and needs.

Social Emotional Health (SEL) Curriculums

It's not possible for everyone to launch a complete SEL curriculum, but if you have flexibility in your schedule a SEL curriculum or even a few activities can be transformative for students. SEL helps students develop skills such as empathy, conflict resolution, and responsible decision-making. When I had complete autonomy over my schedule, we dedicated two hours a week to SEL using a program called Second Step. That's not the only product out there that works, but a SEL curriculum gives you a baseline and frame of reference for students. The curriculum creates norms and a common language that you can build your ecosystem on.

It is important to note that there are some very valid concerns and criticisms of SEL and how it upholds values that center on whiteness. Remember when we talked about white supremacy culture, and that shows up in SEL curriculums as well. If we identify behaviors and values that are good and focus on teaching students how to uphold or demonstrate these values, the values are drawn from a particular cultural narrative. It's important that we understand that values are based on culture and our own frames of reference.

Scholar Dena Simmons writes about decolonizing SEL extensively. Simmons (2021) explains that SEL can be "white supremacy with a hug." Remember that our school system is undergirded by white supremacy culture. Many schools use SEL as a means to make students more compliant and thus adhere more to values that are informed by whiteness.

When teachers decontextualize SEL it can be harmful to their Black and Brown students. Here's an example. We know that at a genetic and intersocial level students of color experience the harms of racism. Teaching students to manage their emotions using SEL, without addressing the reasons that students might be dealing with these emotions, is racial gaslighting. It puts the onus on the student to deal with the implications of all the -isms of society better.

That doesn't mean we throw out learning about our emotions and ourselves. It's the responsibility of the teacher to navigate that two things can be true at the same time. Our student may struggle with relationship building and emotional regulation, but there exists so much in their reality that gives them good reason to be dysregulated.

Cultivate Belonging

Just because students are in a community doesn't mean they feel like they belong. Belonging happens when students are able to bring their full selves to the classroom, including their cultures. It's not about being accepted or tolerated; it's about knowing that you have a place in the community and that your community members see and appreciate you.

I like to use the well-known analogy of a party—from Vernā Myers, an expert in diversity and inclusion (Myers, 2017)—to talk about the differences among diversity, equity, inclusion, and belonging. There are many different iterations, but most go something like this:

- Diversity is when you're invited to a dance party.
- Equity is when everyone is offered a ride to the party and has what they need to get there.
- Inclusion is, once you're at the party, you're asked to dance or play games.
- Belonging is when what the party offers is something you want to experience. Maybe you have dietary restrictions—and the host has special gluten-free or vegan appetizers for you. The DJ is even taking requests for music that people want to hear.

However you arrange the analogy, the idea is that it's not enough to just have diversity in our classrooms or have policies rooted in equity. Kids need to feel like they belong. In the classroom ecosystem, your students might give you feedback in the form of disruptive behaviors if they feel like they don't belong.

As you're outlining the classroom ecosystem, it's not enough to just think about how you will build community. All those routines and systems are wonderful, but how will you help kids feel like they belong?

Have Fun with It!

Building community is supposed to be fun! Teaching is more sustainable when you have a bit of fun with it!

First, ask yourself: are there creative ways that you can build community with your students that intersect with your interests? If being a Pinterest teacher who decks out their classroom in Harry Potter gear feels over the top for you, you can still find ways to bring your personality and personal interests into the classroom.

When I taught at a Catholic parochial school I had some very lively and joyful students. In the mornings while I was putting the finishing touches on the classroom I'd be listening to gospel music while students started trickling in. Over time, more and more students came in early to listen to the music. It was a great opportunity for students to start their day off right, and for us all to do a little bit of bonding.

By November, "Holy Ghost Parties" had become our thing. Throughout the week, students would work to spell out the words *holy ghost*. Each time our community did something well or we had a particularly good instructional block, we'd earn a letter. At the end of the week, if we'd succeeded in spelling out *holy ghost*, we'd have a celebration with Kirk Franklin and other gospel classics. It was such a fun way for us to end the week and bond together. I loved sharing my music with the kids.

It's with these kinds of ideas—these little moments when teachers find that intersection among their interests, the kids' interests, and the needs of the community—that teachers can create a bit of magic with their students.

Highlighting Star Students

Whether you call it student of the week or any other name, highlighting particular students can play a critical role in the classroom ecosystem. This doesn't mean that all the other children in the class aren't also special; in fact, it's ideal to ensure that each student will have the experience at some point. (For younger students especially, you'll want to make sure that all students get a chance to feel celebrated individually.) The star student can have a special chair, have lunch with the teacher, or maybe bring something in from home to share. However it's celebrated, the recognition might be the boost that some of your toughest students need, so look for progress, not perfection.

Peer Mediation

In the lower grades, there can be a million little challenges and problems to deal with each day. This is because these younger students are experiencing the growing pains of learning how to work in community with each other. The good news is that you don't have to get pulled into every dispute over an eraser—students can learn that they can work things out on their own. That's one of the many great things about healthy classroom ecosystems: they build self-sufficiency.

So, consider how you might help your students see themselves as problem-solvers. Especially for lower grades, approaches like peace path and peer mediation can be extremely helpful. Not only do they give students a sense of agency but also they free up the teacher to respond to the high-tier behaviors. And although these approaches might seem daunting, even our youngest learners can take on these roles if they are prepped and given time to learn. Helping kids build problem-solving skills as group members benefits everyone.

IN THE CLASSROOM

Setting yourself up for success starts in the first 10 minutes of class. Experienced teachers might know this that you can see what kind of day you're going to have within the first few minutes of the day.

The First 10 Minutes

The philosophy behind the first 10 minutes is that you're giving your students (and yourself!) a clear road map about how the day is about to proceed. If your students are engaged in the first 10 minutes, then they'll be primed to make it through the entire day. If they step into the classroom and they sense that there's confusion or an opening for chaos, they're going to respond. For example, students who struggle with anxiety might start exhibiting disruptive behaviors because of the uncertainty, and the more high-energy kids might see an opening to get their energy out any way they can.

The First 10 Minutes

The first 10 minutes will define the tone of the classroom. Follow these easy steps to set yourself up for success!

Visuals are essential. Have that anchor chart up, objectives, and timing on the board. Make sure there are visual reminders for students as they enter so they *see* what's going on.

Be ready. Students behave better when the classroom materials are ready. When they walk in, get them straight to work!

Greet. Greet your kids at the door! Acknowledge each one individually. Get a sense of what energy they're bringing to the class.

Review expectations. Be a broken record! Every class period, remind students of who, what, how, and why. Don't leave it up to them to remember your expectations every day.

Check in. As soon as it's possible, check in with the students who struggle. Acknowledge them. Give them a job. Make sure they get *positive* attention early!

The first 10 minutes can go far in setting your instructional block up for success. Preparation is the most important piece of the first 10 minutes. Too frequently teachers don't have the capacity to be prepared because they are so drained from responding to behavior. Then behaviors continue to get worse because teachers haven't adequately prepared. This cycle is broken when teachers get a chance to get ahead and think through their first 10 minutes with intention.

Morning Meetings and Circles

If you've heard negative things about the practice of holding circles in the classroom, know that some schools implement circles in response to a challenge in the community. But that's not their only use. Circles can be a powerful and helpful tool to build up the community and reenforce when things are going well!

Morning meetings are fairly common and standard in elementary classrooms but can certainly have a place with other students as well. At the bare minimum, there should be an opportunity for students in some capacity to check in twice a week with their teacher and each other.

Components of a Great Morning Meeting or Circle

Greeting. This can be simple, such as a welcome message, or more intricate, such as a song. It's the way to notify students that the meeting has begun—the sign that it's time to start the meeting procedures.

(continued)

Sharing. This can look different in each meeting. Sometimes all participants will share; other times only a few. The share could be an opinion, a response, or an emotional check-in.

Group activity. This also varies. Students could read an article, dance, sing a song, learn a new skill—anything that brings the community together in a common goal.

Message. This is your send off. Some teachers do a quote to inspire, a word of the day, or a challenge, something to establish shared language for the day.

I used circles often to unpack big and difficult topics with students, but that is not the only way. Circles can just be an opportunity for discussion about your favorite ice cream flavor. Circles can be preventative or responsive. Preventative circles focus on needs such as classroom routines or community and identity building. Circles can even be incorporated as part of instruction. Responsive circles can be used to address incidents that affect the community.

Remember, regardless of the purpose of your circle, you'll want to spend some time building routines and procedures with students on how the circle will run. It is incredibly discouraging when you have a well-thought-out plan for a circle, but students are not able to experience it fully because there are no norms and boundaries established. (For more, including a comprehensive continuum of restorative practices infographic, check out https://www.learningtogive .org/news/using-restorative-justice-build-school-community.)

Incorporating Mindfulness

Research has shown that mindfulness can improve attention, lower student anxiety, increase compassion, and better regulate emotions (Gerzberg, 2017). There are several ways that mindfulness can be incorporated in your day. Ideally, your entire school would commit to mindfulness as an approach, but if this isn't possible the classroom is a great place to start. Here are some ways you could use mindfulness in the classroom:

- Begin each class with a meditation, starting with 20 seconds and building up to a minute.
- Incorporate a mindful minute as a brain break for students when things get chaotic.
- Bookend transitions between subjects or classes with mindfulness activities such as whole body check-ins, meditations, even coloring!
- Incorporate stretching or even yoga with meditation,

There are many more resources available and even entire curriculums for teachers and classrooms. Some are even free! Mindfulness is a highly transferable skill for students and can help them in their life outside the classroom. Some schools even have hosted workshops or activities for families.

Whole-Class Incentives

We all want to be part of a community, and nothing unifies a classroom community like a goal. An effective strategy to help build a sense of teamwork and pride is to give the classroom a goal to work toward. When I was a classroom teacher, we worked toward activities such as dance parties, pizza parties—even just extra recess time. The students had some metric of measurement, and usually it was something that couldn't be taken away, only added—like marbles to a jar. The exact metric doesn't matter; it just helps students to understand that they are on the same team and working together toward something. The shared and collective purpose helps cultivate belonging.

Individual Incentives

Behavior response is certainly not one size fits all. You might have a strategy that works well with the classroom community but have students who need some extra love or innovation. Some students also may need incentives such as sticker charts or goal setting incorporated into their IEPs.

Here are some best practices to keep in mind:

- Individual incentives, such as points, stickers, tokens, and so on, typically work best when families are aligned with the goals and can support at home what's happening at school.
- The simpler the incentive is the more likely you and the student will be able to stick to it.
- Individual incentives aren't stagnant. After a few months you might need to switch them up.
- Incentives aren't for punishing mistakes; they're about celebrating wins.

Points, Tokens, Prizes

There are many who feel that using extrinsic motivation tools such as points, tokens, and prizes aren't ideal in the classroom. Some teachers are concerned that extrinsic motivation makes kids focus on the reward itself—not on wanting to be a caring member of the classroom ecosystem, just for the sake of the community itself. Many schools, however, recognize that some students might initially need more support, and so require they the use of some kind of token system.

It turns out that there may be a space for points in a healthy ecosystem. For example, my students were arranged in pods of four and they earned pod points for actions such as keeping the space tidy or volunteering to go first. Instead of offering physical rewards I rewarded them with more responsibilities or opportunities to choose partners or first pick for flexible seating. The points weren't taken away, and individual kids weren't singled out. It was a way for them to build their skill set with group dynamics. The key here was that this wasn't my only system. If I only had points, I would end up deducting points when a student made a bad choice, but the group points became a valuable part of our ecosystem.

So points, tokens, and prizes aren't all bad, but there are a few things to consider if you're hoping to use them in some capacity:

- Does the reporting system shame students?
- Are students understanding concepts such as harm, consequences, and community? Or is the motivation completely extrinsic?
- Is the system something you can keep up with and maintain?
- Do you reflect on if you're using the tools equitably?
- Are you using the system in a punitive way?

Most important, though these approaches can work within a healthy ecosystem, in most classrooms they won't work if they're the *only* strategy you're using.

Process Check and Reflection

When something doesn't go well in the classroom, do you think your kids notice? When I debrief with teachers, I often ask them what they thought the kids would say in a debrief. Bringing a level of awareness to your students can help build their agency and their investment in the school community.

Some teachers will designate a process checker: someone to monitor how things go, whether it's during a lesson or a circle. This student reviews the goals or expectations, then tells everyone how they did. When I have particularly chatty students, I often designate them as the process checker: I ask them to monitor how many times someone talks out of turn. It helps them build awareness—and it also just gives them something to do!

Reflection is another powerful tool in the classroom setting. I would have students gather to debrief after lessons that went particularly well or ones that were particularly difficult. In our circle we would talk about the moments when we held up the classroom norms and expectations, as well as the moments when we didn't.

This simple but effective ritual again clarified for everyone that the health of the community wasn't my responsibility but rather the collective responsibility of all members of the community. Students showing up for themselves and others inside their classroom ecosystem will always be more effective than students doing what they think they have to for the sake of following rules.

STAKEHOLDERS WHO SUPPORT YOUR ECOSYSTEM

Many classroom management systems unfortunately dictate that the *only* time a teacher calls a student's parents is when a student misbehaves. But communication with families is essential and should be a regular occurrence to share positive information as well as challenges. The added benefit is that the relationship building of the positive reports will aid any times when you have to report disruptive behavior.

Communicating with Families

If you can, try to develop a system. As a classroom teacher I made calls for no more than 30 minutes on Wednesday and Friday afternoons.

- On Wednesdays I talked with the parents of the students who tended to struggle in my class. That way, if the kid had a rough start to the week, they still had time to turn it around.

- On Fridays I made the good-news reports. I always made sure my last call was positive, so that I didn't head into the weekend hating my job. This was a great way to end my week: I'd connect with a family whom I felt close to or brag about a student who was doing well.

- Outside of this schedule, I'd pepper in additional calls when I could. Quick check-ins can go a long way to build trust and keep your ear to the ground about any issues before they get bigger.

Don't be afraid of technology! There are many apps and systems that you can use to automate emails and texts as well! Also, consider organizing a classroom newsletter if you have the time.

It can be something simple that you just update on a monthly basis—and the end effect can be well worth it.

Make a Plan

Caregivers are part of the ecosystem and need to stay in the loop! You'll want to make a plan for how you'll keep them connected and informed and how you'll continue to build trust with them throughout the year. Some teachers will ask for a room parent or helper who comes in occasionally to help out. Other options are weekly newsletters, a communication system such as Class Dojo or SchoolReach, or even just picking up the phone.

I encourage teachers to always make contact with families in the first few days of school; that way, your first call home or point of contact is guaranteed to be positive. But don't stop there. You may really need a caregiver to trust you down the line, and that will be much easier if you've already established a positive rapport. Emails are great, but if there's a conflict, it's *much* more effective to smooth things over in person. Teachers should also consider creating a survey at the beginning of the year to gather data on families so they know some of their concerns and the best way to communicate with them.

Home Visits

Home visits are a great way to build connections with families. I've worked at many schools that had a regular practice for teachers to visit students' homes to get to know their families. If this is something you'd consider doing, make sure that at the beginning of the year you tell families you'd like to work closely with them and would love to get to know them in their own space. (Typically, families would invite me over for dinner or maybe to some kind of celebration. This all slowed down with COVID-19 concerns, but if both teachers and families feel comfortable this is a great practice to bring back.)

A pitfall to avoid: you aren't there on a data-collection mission. This isn't about psychoanalyzing or pitying a family; it's about building relationship.

Make Deposits

Years ago my bank started a keep the change program to encourage people to save. Basically, they rounded up my credit card purchase to the nearest dollar, and transferred the difference to a savings account that I rarely looked at. When I finally checked it around the holidays, over the course of a year I'd saved $326. Now that's not a life-changing amount of money, but I was excited that I had a few extra dollars to spend on my loved ones (okay, and on myself!).

I like to think about this concept when I map out how I'm going to build connections with students and families. How can I make those little deposits? It's important for all the big things to be there—back to school night, consistent communication, newsletters—but don't forget about the small stuff. A conversation in the car line, a quick text, sharing a photo that you captured. These small moments build up with families and help when you need families to give you the benefit of the doubt.

When teachers share their frustrations with families, it usually boils down to a lack of trust. Let me explain. Over the course of your career you'll almost certainly have one (or many) families who suffer from "my child can do no wrong" syndrome. These are the families who are shocked that their student makes bad choices and will almost certainly question you when you try to bring these concerns to their attention. You'll have families who have a strong distrust for the education system, or families who struggle to trust because of their own issues. It is very challenging to have a healthy classroom ecosystem if you don't have a strong connection with families, so teaming up with these families is essential. Making small deposits can go a long way to grease the wheels in these relationships.

It's the same with students; all the small things certainly add up! Eating lunch with a few students, playing basketball with them during recess, asking them to help you set up your room before class—all of these little interactions help them humanize you, and help you humanize them. Eventually these little deposits will grow.

Parents Shadowing Students

When I shadowed a middle school student for the day, I learned quite a bit about what it felt like to walk the halls from their perspective. It gave me great insight into how I could have better supported them. Admin shadows can be a helpful tool to build empathy for students and troubleshoot to find solutions. I've also worked at schools where family members are invited in to shadow their students.

I had a mother who suffered from my-child-could-do-no-wrong-itis. She had a reason (or excuse) for every behavior her child exhibited. The student habitually bothering other kids? "He was just protecting himself and retaliating." These are the dog ate my homework excuses. It's incredibly difficult to get students to understand accountability when their families won't allow them to experience consequences.

So, one day, exasperated, I invited this mother to come in and shadow her kid for a day. At first he was on his best behavior, and I'm sure she was feeling pretty vindicated. But after lunch the student started to give her a glimpse of the behaviors that had been challenging the classroom community. She was shocked—and she didn't even see the most extreme behaviors!

Because of this we were able to have a much needed real talk afterward and sort out a plan. What was most impactful was the fact that my student saw that I was on a team with his mother and him. If students see that there is a divide between home and school it can be all too easy for students to use this divide to avoid accountability. Instead, we worked on the relationship together.

Taking a Hit for the Team

Sometimes in sports taking a personal loss is something you do for the team (such as a batter taking an out so that the player on third base can score a run). In teaching, there can be many times when maintaining a healthy ecosystem calls for taking a hit for the team.

In my second year of teaching I had a parent whom I struggled to build a relationship with. She was very defensive of her child, very abrupt, and didn't really trust me. I understood her perspective; I, too, would be concerned about a transplant in their early 20s with no teaching credential. We butted heads all the time about her student. He didn't have the worst behavior, but he would openly push back and question me in front of the class. It started off as just being curious and asking good questions, but it quickly turned. He would question everything I did and try to undermine me because of my age. Honestly, it was embarrassing; I could tell he was hearing things at home about me not being effective and was internalizing them. I had a pretty solid administrator that year who navigated the incidents between us very well, but there was one particular time that things got really difficult. We ended up going back and forth about a really small detail, a missing homework assignment. Looking back I can see there were many things wrong with the way I approached the situation. (For example, now I don't even advocate for daily homework in elementary.) At the time I felt like I was right and so did she. Neither of us was budging. I knew her son was lying about a homework assignment, and she was backing the lie.

My principal pulled me aside. He explained that sometimes to build trust and maintain positive relationships you have to take one for the team. What he meant was, even though I knew I was right, and she probably did, too, I had to see the bigger picture. In the grand scheme of things, it was more important that she saw that I was willing to bend and negotiate. There was a lot of school year left, and it didn't make sense for me to just stand on principles for principles' sake. I had to suck it up in this particular incident for the potential of a stronger relationship later. And in the end I was glad I let go about that incident; later that year, the student had a much more serious behavior concern and I needed her support to attend to it. She was much more willing to listen because of how our earlier interaction had ended.

PRACTICES TO KEEP YOUR ECOSYSTEM HEALTHY

Your ecosystem will need maintenance to keep it flourishing. Keep these practices in your back pocket for when things get hectic or challenging in your ecosystem. Remember, a healthy ecosystem doesn't mean that you never need to roll up your sleeves and help your students get back on track from time to time. A healthy ecosystem means that teachers and students know how to navigate challenges with inclusion, joy, and care at the center.

Hard Reset

Sometimes if your technology is glitching you have to turn it off and turn it back on again. The same goes for the classroom ecosystem. A hard reset can look like stopping before things escalate for a brain break or mindfulness minute. Alternatively, you could all just go outside! Sometimes the break is for the whole class, other times it's just for one student. The teacher might even need a break! If there's support staff members to step in for a few minutes that may help you to stabilize.

There are natural ebbs and flows throughout the year. You can use those to your advantage. If you are going on a long break, it's a great time to refresh procedures and introduce new practices into your ecosystem. If you tried a system that isn't landing well with students, a break is a great time to switch things up.

If You Must Ask a Student to Leave the Room

For many reasons, kicking a student out of class should be the absolute last resort. It's also not realistic to think that there'll never be a time when a student might need to step out of the classroom. Here are some questions to ask yourself:

- Where will that student go? Will they be safe? Is there an adult who can de-escalate with them?
- How long will their time away be? How will they know when to come back?
- What will re-entry look like for that student when they return?

Redo and Practice

Practice doesn't need to make perfect but it can make better. It's okay for kids to need practice with how to do school. Remember, there's a good chance that your students have never experienced a "normal" year of schooling because of the impact of the COVID-19 epidemic.

Practicing isn't about forcing compliance but rather about building habits. Asking students to try again or to redo a behavior can also be time-consuming and requires patience. For most students, you'll only need to do this in the first few weeks of school a few times, and they'll be good with just occasional reminders. With other students this is something that you'll have to do over and over, but it's an easy, nonpunitive way to help them build good community habits.

You've probably seen this modeled plenty of times: the teacher uses an attention grabber, some kind of call and response, and then only 50% of students follow along. In situations like this and many more it's okay to encouragingly ask students to try again.

Avoid Power Struggles

Let's take for example when you want all the students to follow a cue, but there's one who doesn't participate. The first thing you should question is why. Is that student being intentionally disruptive? Or are they having some kind of issue?

If you have a student who likes attention, the worst thing you can do is give them a stage. You absolutely do not want to get into a one-on-one showdown with a child—especially when all the other kids are watching—for several reasons:

- If the student wants attention, you're giving them what they want and reinforcing the behavior.
- If you're in a showdown with a student, you've already lost because now it becomes about showing who's in charge, which models a toxic relationship within the ecosystem.
- All the other students are now seeing if they want some one-on-one attention all they have to do is act out.
- When you're in those heated moments, you're more likely to snap to a punishment to scare the child without really thinking about what makes sense.

Sometimes when I'm observing classrooms a teacher will give an instruction that's really simple, such as "turn to page 4." If a student doesn't follow along, the teacher will jump automatically to a list of ultimatums. "If you don't do _____ then no recess!" "If you don't do ___ then you're going to the principal's office!" and it becomes a back and forth. Unfortunately, it's the teacher who is losing in this scenario. Once you give out a consequence you really should stick to it—or else all your subsequent warnings will be ignored—and before you know it, a child is talking to the principal about why they didn't turn to page 4.

What should you do instead? You could approach the student for a calm check-in. In some scenarios it might be helpful to transition the rest of the class, then help that student move to an activity that they can do independently.

Remember, once you're in a public power struggle with a student, you've already lost. Instead, take a pause until you can have a more substantive conversation with your student.

Talk It Out

You'd be surprised how infrequently some of our students have the undivided attention of an adult. An unintended consequence of technology is that our students have fewer in-person interactions with the world around them; instead, they are focused on a screen. When I reflect on the changes that I've seen since I started teaching, I see a clear difference in the amount of time that students spend interacting with people around them. Technology makes it just too easy. Caregivers are just people so they themselves struggle with screen time and the generation of kids in our classrooms now might have grown up watching iPads in the car, at the supermarket, and/or even at the dinner table. This is by no means a judgment against families and care givers. The US culture is demanding and is not set up to allow families time to be with each other. Because of economic insecurity, climate injustice, police brutality, and a tumultuous political landscape (to name just a few!) our capacity has never been lower.

What does this mean for kids? Kids need to interact, to question, and to explore. Sure, some of the behaviors students exhibit in class might be just to get your attention. But always keep in mind that maybe they just need to talk! Never underestimate the power of one-on-ones with a student.

Don't Rush

It's going to be challenging, but you can give yourself a time-out. What I mean is that you don't have to snap and react to something right away. You can take some time to process and come up with a better strategy.

In my own middle school classroom I used this frequently. One of the behaviors I struggled with most was students making racist or misogynistic comments. It's important to always acknowledge that you hear these comments, even if you don't know what exactly to say. In those moments I'd say something like, "I want to just be clear that I heard that and we are going to address it both individually and as a community, but not at this exact moment. But it wasn't okay." That gave me time to gather myself and outline a plan. If you don't know what to say in the moment, you could accidentally end up either trivializing the comment or not fully addressing the harm.

You can also give yourself or the student a time-out. We want kids in class as much as possible but there are certainly times where extreme behaviors mean our students need to take a break. Breaks are a very helpful and valid de-escalation strategy. If you find yourself in a tense situation with a student, a timed and supervised break can be incredibly helpful. I've seen teachers get very creative with this. Sometimes kids need to feel a little extra attention or feel important. A nonessential (or even completely made up!) errand can do the trick.

If you rush to dole out a consequence, you might be responding with emotion or escalation instead of from a place of wellness and wholeness. Take the time you need to respond intentionally.

Ask Yourself Why

This might be the most important question that you ask yourself when it comes to behavior. You have to understand the antecedents and the motivations for your students. In a classroom that I was visiting in California a 3rd-grade teacher was struggling with wanderers and off-task students. She had wanted to move away from forcing her kids to "sit in STAR" and let them have a bit more flexibility with their bodies, but she was regretting her decision because they were very wiggly during her direct instruction. If you're not familiar with STAR, it stands for sitting up, listening, asking and answering questions, and raising your hand. The acronym has become fairly common place in schools. The intention is to encourage students to be actively engaged. In reality, it usually ends up being yet another way to police students' bodies. During the observation I asked her permission to film her and she agreed. She was frustrated that three students got out of their seats and at least two side conversations popped up. As we watched the lesson back she realized that she had been essentially talking at the students for a solid 14 minutes before anyone else had a chance to speak. Developmentally, her 3rd graders were not ready to sit in direct instruction for that long, so although their behaviors did distract the few students who were trying their very best to listen, we realized that it wasn't a reasonable ask. If we didn't examine the why, those students would have lost a privilege or had their clip moved up or down. Understanding the why is a critical proactive approach because it gives the teacher an opportunity to respond to a behavior before it even happens.

When a student is exhibiting behaviors habitually, it can be incredibly enlightening to try and figure out what type of feedback they're giving you. Are they telling you that they need you to chunk your instruction? Are they communicating that they don't feel ready to approach an academic task? Are they hungry? Tired? On edge because they know a transition is coming? As kids are learning how to manage their own thoughts and emotions, they might simply be communicating with you in ineffective ways.

Even the older kids struggle to communicate sometimes. I worked with some middle school teachers in Colorado who were struggling with behavior. They had some dejected students that they just couldn't get to. They were difficult to build relationships with because they weren't open to talking with teachers—they just shuffled in and out of their classes. They weren't harming other students, but they were checked out. As a last ditch effort, I shadowed them for a day. Here's what I noticed: from the beginning of the day at 7:54 to the end of their day at 3:12, they had no positive interactions with adults. Even worse: when they came in with their heads down and hoods on, someone yelled at them to take them off. This was the first interaction in their day. In their first class, when they weren't immediately responsive to the teacher, they were threatened with detention. At lunch they had hushed interactions with their peers, but were redirected because they were hovering near the field. By the last class one of the boys was totally unresponsive. He sat quietly and doodled anime characters. By the end of the day no adult had even addressed them by name. No greeting when they walked in to class. No one asked them about their day, their life. They got nothing but directions and redirections. This was a middle school, so it wasn't the fault of one individual teacher, or even the staff as a whole. But seeing the day through the eyes of a student gave me a new perspective about their why. Why weren't these kids responsive? They had been psychologically beaten down by adults all day!

This is a pretty extreme example, but it reveals the power of asking why. When you find yourself frustrated with your students' behavior, before you jump to a punishment, ask why.

Using Setbacks as Opportunities

I was at my healthiest, clocking in well above the recommended 10,000 steps, when I was a dean—and not to mention the school had stairs. I had my walkie-talkie, and I spent at least three hours a day running and responding between classrooms. Giving kids a break, giving teachers a break, having quick chats in the hallway, leading mindful minutes, and of course listening to my fair share of middle school drama. It might sound ironic, but the kids whom I talked to the most, the ones with the worst behavior, were the kids whom I had the strongest relationships with. They knew all about me, I knew all about them. They saw what I was eating for lunch (because half the time I was running around with it) and they knew about my secret stash of Milano cookies (for the teachers, not the students).

It didn't occur to me until it was too late that I was actually doing my teachers a disservice by swooping in so frequently. I was getting to know these wonderfully complex little people so well in all the time they spent *outside* of the classrooms.

In my second year, I decided to switch things up. I told my teachers that I was going to be just as responsive, but, assuming that the student is not a danger to themselves or others, I wouldn't be taking them out. Instead, I'd sit with the class, picking up wherever they left off, and have the teacher take the break with the student. This wasn't possible for all my teachers all the time—some just didn't have the experience or the emotional stability—but for my teachers who were ready, this worked wonders!

With this approach, the teacher got to see the student calm down, hear the funny stories about what they did last night, and argue about their favorite video game character. Remember how it's good to consider the students' why? Well, with some of these kids the why was that they wanted to have some kind of interaction with their teacher—they just didn't know how to ask for it. These short little chats or walks helped them build that bond.

I also stepped in when teachers just needed a break. We cannot talk about seeing our students' humanity without also seeing our teachers' humanity as well; when you're in the trenches, trying your best to respond with humanity, you're giving your energy. It's absolutely acceptable to ask for a break from time to time. When teacher take a break it has the added advantage of giving your administrator a chance to interact with your students.

Setbacks can be incredibly frustrating, but they can be turned into meaningful opportunities.

Best Practices in Accountability

When you hold students accountable for their behaviors in the classroom (Figure 5.3), consider the three As: admit, apologize, act.

Admit can be the most difficult step for students. Kids are so used to being criminalized and punished in the classroom that their immediate reaction sometimes is to lie as opposed to admitting that they've made a mistake. Any time I have a student who doesn't admit their behaviors, I reflect on the existing relationship that I have with the student. Did I create a space where they feel safe to make mistakes? Did the student feel that they could be honest and authentic with me?

Usually, if they're lying they're afraid of the consequences. Developmentally, kids learn to navigate tough situations and tell the truth, but it's much easier when the classroom culture is one that makes mistakes okay. Sometimes, when kids are caught in a lie, their immediate response is to double down and stick with the lie. If this is the case, sometimes you just need to give them some time to de-escalate so that they can start being honest.

Apologizing is an important step in healing for the community. Although it's just words, an apology can go far in repair. Remember we are seeking to repair harm and restore the community, not just punish students

Figure 5.3 Best Practices for Accountability

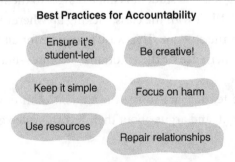

Best Practices for Accountability

Ensure it's student-led

Be creative!

Keep it simple

Focus on harm

Use resources

Repair relationships

The act step too often falls by the wayside in the classroom. It is critical that students understand that they need to take action after experiencing consequences. Often with my middle school students I would particularly emphasize this step. Middle school is when students are learning a deeper appreciation of boundaries and reconciliation. Students need to understand that if their behavior harms their community, they need to change the behaviors.

When you're holding students accountable, remember the three As.

Offer Students Fresh Starts

One of the benefits of staying at a school long term is that you get to develop a deep bond or connection with students or families. Students change in both physical appearance and disposition so it can be a great joy to watch kids grow up and see how their personality shifts and develops over time. It is critical that kids are given the grace and space to change and grow.

Even the students whom you think you know very well might surprise you. That is why I caution teachers who rely heavily on the experience and opinions of other teachers. Teachers sharing information between each other can be very helpful. You can get advice on how to work best with families or gather insight about your students. But there is a fine line between sharing insights about students and focusing on deficit narratives.

Kids need fresh starts. They need to understand that their past mistakes won't mean they can never expect future success. It can be difficult to truly give a student a clean slate in the classroom if you're subscribing heavily to the narrative that they're a behavior problem.

What's even worse is that students can start to internalize these narratives about themselves. Sometimes students who are repeatedly identified as "behavior problems" push back and try to break out of this perception. Other times, they dig even deeper into this identity. If you are going to get insight from other teachers, make sure that you are still allowing yourself to be open to growth and progress from your students.

You might be in a space of emotion or escalation, but it's important to take care of yourself to ensure you'll be able to give your students fresh starts within the school day. When a student has a rough morning, it doesn't necessarily mean they'll have a rough afternoon. You might need to take a break, take a walk, or grab a treat from the break room to give yourself some space to decompress. A tense Monday with a student can easily turn into an amazing Wednesday to Friday if you're able to give your student a fresh start.

Progress over Perfection

If you have students with severe behavior challenges, you'll have to remember that sometimes you have to concede the small things to work toward the ultimate goal. My first time as a dean wasn't easy. I often told folks that it was the worst job in the school. I almost exclusively talked to the students with major behavior challenges all day. I rarely got to do the fun stuff. Even during pep rallies I was the person who had to sit with the kids who weren't allowed to participate. In hindsight, we all should have been at the pep rally, because further isolating a student who's acting out because they don't feel like they're part of the community is not productive. But in this particular job, I inherited many policies that I didn't agree with ideologically. My day-to-day usually consisted of running between classrooms to respond to teacher needs and de-escalate students. I had a particularly challenging student who liked to destroy classrooms and tear down bulletin boards. This is a particularly tough behavior for teachers. Not only is it disruptive but also teachers pour a significant amount of work and time and heart into their boards. This student would tear down boards from his own classroom and any in his path.

It was Thursday, and this student had had quite the week. It was constant break down after break down. The student had a one-on-one aide, but if you're familiar with students with tier 3 and sometimes dangerous behaviors, you'll understand an aide is only trained to do so much. When I was called into the classroom the student was breaking color pencils, actually a fairly minor behavior based on what I'd seen in the past. After taking turns trying to talk to the student and get through to him, he eventually calmed down and did some belly breaths. When he was calmer, it was different than other times he'd come out of a rage before. He offered to clean up, apologized to the teachers and the other students, and according to the counselor did great in his therapy session. He was walking out of the office and I was about to walk him back to class. I couldn't help but feel proud of him. Here was this 7-year-old victim of abuse modeling accountability and empathy better than some adults!

It was at this moment that I made what would become a very controversial decision. We went outside for 10 minutes of extra recess time. Now, 10 minutes doesn't sound like a lot for an adult, but to a kid it's a lifetime. When we came back inside, many of the other teachers were shocked. This student did not have a good day by the metrics that we used. And he had an even worse week. For any other student, I probably would have called his parents a long time ago. But the goal here isn't perfection, it's progress. If I used the metrics that I was using for all the other students this kid would be perpetually in the negative. Every day would be a bad day. So you have to be strategic and see the bigger picture with some students. You also want to build momentum. Fridays were his worst days. If I could get him moving in a positive direction on Thursday, maybe Friday would be good, too. But it was more than that. For kids who are perpetually "that kid," the behavior problem whom all the teachers talk about, they rarely get to experience all the great things about school. They don't get to make the fun memories on the playground and all of the extra morale boosters that other kids get to participate in. If you have a student who gives you a difficult time, and they start to show you progress, you have to seize the opportunity to celebrate them. This can be difficult for teachers because they have to let go of the past behavior. Sometimes that behavior specifically targets them! That's why it's so important to offer students fresh starts.

Major disclaimer here. It's not always the right call. Remember, this was a 2nd grader who hadn't physically harmed anyone, just things. This is definitely a case-by-case call, but if you have a student who turns their day around, is open to being accountable, and accepts the consequences, you might want to celebrate the progress instead of waiting for perfection.

Shoot for a Winning Record

I don't watch a lot of sports, but I have some friends and family who are really into them and sometimes I'll watch along. I was watching a basketball team that some of my friends closely follow throughout the season. From my vantage point, this team was doing awfully. They lost all the games I watched. When I mentioned this my friend replied, "Don't worry, they're still above 500." This basically means that they have a winning record. As long as they win more than they lose and stay above 500, they're okay.

That really stuck with me, and it's something that I talk to my teachers about all the time. When you're in the day-to-day, it might not seem like you're making a ton of progress. You might feel like you're losing. But take a step back and consider: how's your overall record? As long as you have more days when you make some progress than days when you can't score any points, you still have a winning record.

Troubleshooting When You've Tried Everything

Let's say you've tried everything and your ecosystem still isn't flourishing. Let's look at a few reasons why this might be the case:

Unaddressed harm. Remember, relationships can't be healed through just punishments, even consequences. When someone harms another person in your ecosystem, the harm must be addressed. This can be done with a conversation, a circle, or other forms of structured communication, but it must take place for students to move forward.

Unexamined bias. As the teacher, it is absolutely critical that you are doing your internal work. We've talked about this concept quite a bit in this book, but it's worth addressing again. If you aren't aware of how your own bias is showing up in the classroom, you might be missing opportunities to try new or different things in the classroom ecosystem. Working through your own biases can also help you understand how other systemic barriers are affecting your students.

Things take time. It's not always the easiest answer, but sometimes your students just need more time. They need to get into patterns and establish routines with each other. If your students are unlearning problematic practices it might take even more time for students to get used to new expectations. Sometimes it just takes a while before things click.

Your ecosystem is a complex web of interactions and relationships between students, teachers, and stakeholders. It'll be messy, chaotic, and loud at times. The critical mindset shift that we must make is that a joyful, caring, and inclusive classroom might not look like kids sitting perfectly still at their desks all day. Instead look to things like meaningful relationships, a sense of belonging, and students who are actively engaged in their learning as indicators of a thriving ecosystem.

CONCLUSION

When I first started teaching, I made so many mistakes. I didn't have much training on behavior management. I didn't study education in under-grad, so I had to learn everything from my emergency credentialing program. It was quite a trial-and-error type of learning curve. I did the best with what I knew at the time, but if I'm honest, my classroom started out as rather carceral. I believed in building community, but I just didn't have the creative mind to fig-ure out how to create a joyful and equitable classroom.

In those days, many people in the education sphere weren't talking about equity work the way we do now. Instead it was more about "culturally responsive teaching." I found many ways to be culturally responsive that I was proud of in my instruction. I had protagonists of color in my library, people of color on the walls, and I wasn't shy about calling out problematic ideas and notions in the textbooks. But I was still not yet thinking about my behavior response and my behavior management.

Slowly, as I learned, more things started to shift. It started first with just a few things, trying different strategies, incorporating more circles, but I didn't really see the changes that I was looking for until I shifted my mindset. It took me accepting first that I was in fact perpetuating harm in those early days. I had to realize that even though my intent was never to harm my students, my behavior management practices were in fact harmful.

I wanted better for my students, so I read books, listened to podcasts, and watched videos. I soaked it all up, until one day it just clicked. It clicked when I realized that I had to unlearn everything that I thought I knew about behavior management. I had to unlearn what it meant to be a "well-behaved" student in my classroom.

I still learn every day. Every time I enter a new classroom I see teachers who are responding to very difficult circumstances in new and unique ways. The "-isms" are so deeply ingrained in our systems that it takes active work to push up against them. It's not easy, but I see and hear about teachers doing it every day!

That's what I love about this work. I see the brilliance and resilience of teachers every day. Teachers have always been steadfast in their dedication to their students, regardless of the many obstacles. We find a way, or we make one.

These past few years have brought unprecedented challenges. Many teachers have walked away from the profession for good. I don't blame them.

A change is long overdue. I hope that this book can be one small piece of the puzzle that stakeholders across the country are putting together as we try and get education back on track.

Building a classroom ecosystem rooted in joy, belonging, and care won't happen overnight, and it won't be easy. There is no one-size-fits-all solution with classroom culture. Even if you implement all these strategies perfectly to the letter, you might still have some rough days, and that's okay! Ecosystems are not stagnant—they're noisy and chaotic and full of life. In the challenging moments you can revisit some of the strategies in this book. The year has natural ebbs and flows, and each year gets easier because you have a better idea of what to expect. As the teacher, it's up to you to be as proactive as possible and use your toolbox when it's time to get reactive. Each year you'll learn new things about teaching and about yourself.

Part of getting education means fighting for the systemic changes that'll make teaching more sustainable for adults, and more joyful for students. The work of advocating for smaller class sizes, more mental health support, and better pay, just to name a few needed changes, continues.

Until then, why do we stay in this profession when there are easier, better-paying, and certainly less-stressful options out there? Teaching is not a job; it's a vocation and a calling. We are called to a higher purpose of being in community with our students. We know we deserve better, so we find the meaningful moments among the chaos while we fight for something better.

So, what's next for you? I hope that reading this book will be only the beginning of your journey. I hope you'll return to the classroom with renewed fervor. This isn't just head work, it's heart work. It requires a commitment to justice, to not taking the easy way out. You have an amazing opportunity. The change to be a part of dismantling harmful systems and reimagining and rebuilding something new. Something better. Something rooted in joy, belonging, and care.

EPILOGUE: WHERE ARE THEY NOW?

Many of the teachers I talked about in this book are my dear friends and are still in the classroom. A few, like Norah and Ms. Benning, left the field. I get it. Teaching just isn't for everyone.

I owe quite a bit of gratitude to the teachers whom I've worked with throughout my career. Whether they were my mentors or my coachees, they taught me so much.

I also owe a great debt to my students. I hope you now feel like you know some of my students almost as well as I do. I always get questions about where they are now, so I'll take this opportunity to give you some updates.

Johnny was one of the most challenging students I worked with in my career. Whenever I saw him at school in the years after he was my student, we laughed about all those times. I'm glad to say that time gave me a sense of humor about all the challenges I faced every year. After Johnny left school we lost touch, but recently I found out through one of his friends that he moved away and is doing well. He's had some bumps, but he's planning to go to college somewhere in California.

I'd lost touch with **Celia** for years until, just a few months before writing this book, she found me on TikTok! She sent me the sweetest message, telling me that she remembered me as strict, but that she knew I cared about her. I shed a few tears reading that message. She's doing well at a prestigious high school and her favorite subject is Social Studies.

Emily has had a rough time since the last time I saw her. The instability that she experienced at home was only made worse by the pandemic. Her attendance is spotty, and she still has some progress to make both academically and behaviorally. But her teachers and school leaders seem better equipped to support her.

Remember, they're not all happy endings. **Martin** was in a particularly rough middle-school class, and he and many of his cohort still struggle to this day. Some were expelled from the school where I'd worked; and some I've lost touch with completely. I still hold out hope. Sometimes you have to play the long game.

A few students from that group are doing well. They've all either graduated from high school (or will soon), and some blossomed into joyful, happy, and healthy young adults.

Hailey is thriving at a small private high school. She's a cheerleader and wants to go into communications, which she will absolutely thrive at.

Ronni is still just as boisterous and jovial and is very active on social media. Last time we talked she told me she still doesn't like school, but I hold out hope that she'll regain that joy eventually.

REFERENCES

Abramson, A. (2022). Children's mental health in crisis. *2022 Trends Report, 53*(1), 69.

ACLU. (2020). School-to-prison pipeline. *Juvenile Justice.* https://www.aclu.org/issues/juvenile-justice/school-prison-pipeline/school-prison-pipeline

Berwick, C. (2019). What does the research say about standardized testing? *Edutopia* (October 25). https://www.edutopia.org/article/what-does-research-say-about-testing/

Bhat, J. (2017). Attention spans in the age of technology. National Alliance on Mental Illness (August 14). https://www.nami.org/Blogs/NAMI-Blog/August-2017/Attention-Spans-in-the-Age-of-Technology

Brown, B. (2012). Listening to shame. *TED* (March 16). YouTube video, 20:38. https://www.youtube.com/watch?v=psN1DORYYV0

Buchanan, L., & Bui, Q. (2020, July 3). Black Lives Matter may be the biggest social movement in history. *New York Times.* https://www.nytimes.com/interactive/2020/07/03/us/george-floyd-protests-crowd-size.html

Camera, L. (2021). Study confirms school-to-prison pipeline. *US News* (July 27).

Center on Education Policy. (2020). History and evolution of public education in the US. Graduate School of Education & Human Development, George Washington University. https://files.eric.ed.gov/fulltext/ED606970.pdf

Chin, M. J., Quinn, D. M., Dhaliwal, T. K., & Lovison, V. S. (2020). Bias in the air: A nationwide exploration of teachers' implicit racial attitudes, aggregate bias, and student outcomes. *Educational Researcher, 49*(8). https://doi.org/10.3102/0013189X20937240

Chow, K. (2017). Who can call themselves "Brown"? *NPR Code Switch* (December 11).

Coristine, S., Russo, S., Fitzmorris, R., Beninato, P., & Rivolta, G. (2022, April 1). The importance of student-teacher relationships. *Classroom Practice in 2022.* https://ecampusontario .pressbooks.pub/educ5202/chapter/the-importance-of-student-teacher-relationships/

Epstein, R., Blake, J., & Gonzalez, T. (n.d.). Girlhood interrupted: The erasure of Black girls' childhood. Center on Poverty and Inequality, Georgetown Law. https://genderjustice andopportunity.georgetown.edu/wp-content/uploads/2020/06/girlhood-interrupted.pdf

Fensterwald, J. (2022). California does little to ensure all kids read by the third grade. *EdSource Special Report* (August 26).

Gerzberg, C. O. (2017). Best practices for bringing mindfulness into schools. *Mindful.* https:// www.mindful.org/mindfulness-in-education/

Ginwright, S. (2018). The future of healing: Shifting from trauma informed care to healing centered engagement. https://ginwright.medium.com/the-future-of-healing-shifting-from-trauma-informed-care-to-healing-centered-engagement-634f557ce69c

Ginwright, S. (2022). *The Four pivots: Reimagining justice, reimagining ourselves.* North Atlantic Press.

Hacker, C., Zalani A., Sanchez, J., & Stock, S. (2022). Handcuffs in hallways: Hundreds of elementary students arrested at U.S. schools. *CBS News* (December 9). https://www.cbsnews .com/news/hundreds-of-elementary-students-arrested-at-us-schools/

Hammond, Z. (2014). *Culturally responsive teaching and the brain: Promoting authentic engagement and rigor among culturally and linguistically diverse students.* Corwin.

Harvard Health. (2020). Understand the stress response. *Staying Healthy* (July 6). https://www .health.harvard.edu/staying-healthy/understanding-the-stress-response

Healy, M. (2016). Eye-tracking technology shows that preschool teachers have implicit bias against Black boys. *Los Angeles Times* (September 28).

Human Rights Council. (2022). Human rights campaign condemns Florida Board of Education for approving shameful, discriminatory measures targeting LGBTQ+ students and teachers. Press release (October 19). https://www.hrc.org/press-releases/human-rights-campaign-condemns-florida-board-of-education-for-approving-shameful-discriminatory-measures-targeting-lgbtq-students-and-teachers

Jackson, C. (2021). What is redlining? *New York Times* (August 17).

Jones, K., & Okun, T. (2001). *From dismantling racism: A workbook for social change groups.* Minnesota Historical Society.

King, E. (2022). Why classroom clip charts do more harm than good. *Parents Magazine* (May 17).

Kinzler, K. (2016). How kids learn prejudice. *New York Times* (October 21).

Kleinfeld, J. (February 1975). Effective teachers of Eskimo and Indian students. *School Review*, 83(2), 301–344.

Krause, K. H., Verlenden, J. V., Szucs, L. E., et al. (2021). Disruptions to school and home life among high school students during the COVID-19 pandemic—Adolescent Behaviors and Experiences Survey, United States. *MMWR Suppl 2022*, 71(Suppl-3), 28–34. http://dx.doi .org/10.15585/mmwr.su7103a5

Ladson-Billings, G. (2009). *The dreamkeepers* (2nd ed.). Jossey-Bass.

Lewin, T. (2012) Black students face more discipline data suggests. *New York Times* (March 6).

Loewus, L. (2021). Why teachers leave—or don't: A look at the numbers. *Edweek* (May 4).

Losen, D., & Whitaker, A. (2017). Lost instructions: The disparate impact of the school discipline gap in California. *The Civil Rights Project* (October 24). https://www.civilrights project.ucla.edu/resources/projects/center-for-civil-rights-remedies/school-to-prison-folder/summary-reports/lost-instruction-the-disparate-impact-of-the-school-discipline-gap-in-california

Love, Bettina L. (2019). *We want to do more than survive*. Beacon.

Marshall, J. (2012). *Common schools movement*. SAGE.

Martin, J. (2022). The 50 most banned books in America. *CBS News* (10 January). https://www .cbsnews.com/pictures/the-50-most-banned-books-in-america/

Maryam, A. (2022). How has technology impacted the attention span of students. *The Companion* (November 21). https://thecompanion.in/how-has-technology-impacted-the-attention-spans-of-students

Mazzei, P., Hartocollis, A. (2023). Florida rejects A.P African American Studies class. *New York Times* (January 19).

Myers, Vernā. (2017). Diversity doesn't stick without inclusion. The Vernā Myers Company. https://www.vernamyers.com/2017/02/04/diversity-doesnt-stick-without-inclusion/

National Center for Education Statistics. (2020). Race and ethnicity of public school teachers and their students. https://nces.ed.gov/pubs2020/2020103/index.asp

National Center for Learning Disabilities. (2020). Significant disproportionality in special education trends among Black students. https://www.ncld.org/wp-content/ uploads/2020/10/2020-NCLD-Disproportionality_Black-Students_FINAL.pdf

National Education Association. (2021). Asset-based, student-centered learning environments (November 16). https://nea.certificationbank.com/images/NEAdocuments/DECC/ NEA_DEC6.pdf

NEA Center for Social Justice. (2020). White supremacy culture resources (December). https:// www.nea.org/resource-library/white-supremacy-culture-resources

Okonofua, J., & Eberhardt, J. (2015). Two strikes: Race and the disciplining of young students. *Psychological Science, 26*(5).

PACE. (2018). What is California's high school graduation rate? Policy Analysis for California Education Report. https://edpolicyinca.org/sites/default/files/HS_Grad_Rate_online.pdf

Paris, D., & Alim, S. (2017). *Culturally sustaining pedagogies: Teaching and learning for justice in a changing world*. Teachers College Press.

Pierson, R. (2013, May). Every kid needs a champion. *TED*. https://www.ted.com/speakers/rita_f_pierson

Reuters Staff. (2016) Black students more likely to be suspended: U.S. Education Department. *Reuters* (June 7).

Riddle, T., & Sinclair, S. (2019). Racial disparities in school-based disciplinary actions are associated with county-level rates of racial bias. *PNAS Proceedings of the National Academy of Sciences of the United States of America, 116*(17), 8255–8260. https://doi.org/10.1073/pnas.1808307116

Sawchuk, S. (2021) School resource officers (SROs) explained. *EdWeek* (November 16).

Simmons, D. (2021). Why SEL alone isn't enough. *ASCD, 78*(6). https://www.ascd.org/el/articles/why-sel-alone-isnt-enough

Stinson, P. (2021). Texas Senate votes to remove required lessons on civil rights. *Bloomberg Law* (July 26). https://news.bloomberglaw.com/social-justice/texas-senate-votes-to-remove-required-lessons-on-civil-rights

Tatum, B. D. (2017). *Why are all the Black kids sitting together in the cafeteria?* Basic Books.

U.S. Bureau of Labor Statistics. (2021). American time use survey. https://www.bls.gov/tus/

US Department of Health and Human Services. (2021). National healthcare quality and disparities report. https://www.ahrq.gov/sites/default/files/wysiwyg/research/findings/nhqrdr/2019qdr.pdf

U.S. Department of Justice. (2016). Disabilities reported by prisoners. Survey of prison inmates. https://bjs.ojp.gov/content/pub/pdf/drpspi16st.pdf

Watson, T. (2019). Revealing and uprooting cellular violence: Black men and the biopsychosocial impact of microaggressions. ProQuest.

Waxman, O. (2022). Anti-"critical race theory" laws are working. Teachers are thinking twice about how they talk about race. *Time* (June 30).

Williams, P. (2022). The right-wing mothers fueling the school board wars. *The New Yorker* (October 31).

GLOSSARY

ableist   institutional and interpersonal discrimination and/or prejudice against individuals with disabilities.

anti-racism/anti-bias   a stance of striving to dismantle racist practices.

asset pedagogies   Anti-racism, as it pertains to education, is part of a larger pedagogical approach that is sometimes comprehensively referred to as *asset pedagogies*. There are many asset pedagogies, but the unifying concept is that we see our students from an asset lens. According to the National Education Association (2021), asset pedagogies focus on the unique strengths that our students bring to the classroom.

BIPOC   Black, Indigenous, or person of color.

Black and Brown   racial classification typically referring to self-identifying Black people and people of color.

code-switching   adjusting one's behavior and demeanor in order to assimilate into one's environment. (In linguistics the term refers to switching languages or dialects within one conversation.)

critical race theory (CRT)   an academic, social, and legal concept and framework that is grounded in the idea that although race is a social construct, it is deeply embedded in all institutions in the United States. CRT contends that institutions are intentionally designed to continue to exploit and oppress people of color.

culturally relevant pedagogy (CRP)   a pedagogical approach that seeks to focus on multiple facets of student success and achievement while supporting and upholding student culture and identity.

DEI diversity, equity, and inclusion—often used in relation to large-scale efforts made with the goal of promoting diversity, equity, and inclusion of a heterogenous population (such as within a school or workplace).

emergent bilingual a student in the process of learning formalized English in the school setting. Other commonly used terms are *English language learner* or *ELL*.

equity work a broad term to refer to the pursuit of practices and policies that promote equity within a school or organization.

ESL (English as a second language) earlier terminology for *emergent bilingual*; some districts still use this terminology.

IEP (individualized education plan) a legal document that is designed to ensure that a child with a disability receives support and services to help them thrive. IEPs are codesigned with families, special education teachers, general education teachers. and service providers.

neurotypical refers to a person who has the brain processes, functions, and behaviors that would be described as "typical" or standard.

PD (professional development) the time is set aside for teachers to continue to develop their teaching praxis.

Social and emotional learning (SEL) a methodology that seeks to equip students with the skills to understand their own emotions, show empathy for others, and have a healthy relationship with their own mental health.

social justice a doctrine of egalitarianism whereby all members of society have equal access to privilege and opportunity.

ABOUT THE AUTHOR

Deonna Smith is a native of Spokane, Washington, and a current Angeleno. Deonna's upbringing in a well-meaning but very homogenous town was an early catalyst for her passion for educational justice. As a student, Deonna struggled to navigate an education system that just wasn't designed for students like her: Black, low-income, and first-generation college-bound. With hard work and a lot of luck, Deonna was able to make it into Gonzaga University for undergrad and Notre Dame for her masters. It was here her career trajectory began to take shape. Deonna studied political science, Spanish, and international studies but really found her vocation in her master's of education program. As a fresh alumna, Deonna started off her teaching career in an elementary school in Oakland, California. Working with "challenging" and "urban" students was not what you often see on TV and on social media. The students in the "tough" neighborhoods were bright, creative, and hilarious! So Deonna continued to work in underfunded schools and with students that the education system had all but given up on. It was during this time that she began to cultivate and refine her skills as an educator. Her vision was simple: focus on relationships, have an asset mindset, and always see education as liberation. Before long, opportunities to coach and support other teachers presented themselves and Deonna eventually became an administrator. Always a life-long learner, Deonna knew that the next logical step would be entering a doctoral program to continue to fine-tune her praxis as an educator; she earned her doctorate in education in 2022. Deonna has expanded her network to include more than 100,000 followers on social media who are passionate about anti-racism as well. Recently, folks have taken notice. Deonna is the 2022 winner of the Social Justice Award through Edu Choice and was recently featured in BuzzFeed and *Forbes*. Through her platforms, Deonna provides tips, frameworks, and other resources for teachers who are interested in this work. When not working on her consulting business or online community, Deonna loves baking and hiking.

INDEX

B

Bandwidth, problems, 101, 106
Bathroom passes, usage, 68
Behavior
    bias, relationship, 18, 82–85
    big behaviors, asset-based lens (need), 86
    challenges, 152
    cultural derivation, 85f
    culture, relationship, 85
    cumulativeness, 51
    disruptiveness, 59
    feedback, equivalence, 51–52
    frustration, 72
    management, 43–45, 70
        practices, 155–156
    occurrence, 52
    perception, reframing, 26
    problems, 151
    responses
        need, 59
        troubleshooting, 116
Belonging, cultivation, 134
Best intentions, assumption, 50–51
Bias
    appearance, 83
    behavior, relationship, 18, 82–85
    cultural biases, 21
    unexamined bias, 153
Bigotry, impact, 31
Black and Brown
    children
        joy, experience, 122–123
        overrepresentation, 87
    people
        harm/racism, 5–6
        oppression systems, unlearning, 70
    phrase, 4
    racial classification, 161
Black and Brown students
    difficulties, 119
    police murders, 92

    success, 33
    treatment, 84–85
Black, Indigenous, or person of color (BIPOC), 4,
        68, 112–113, 161
    children, 32
Books, banning, 3
Boundaries
    crossing, teacher fear, 103
    navigation, 102–103
    student understanding, fun (increase), 121
Brain drain, 117
Brown, Brené, 13

C

Caregivers, impact, 147
Cell phone expectations (classroom
        procedure), 131
Challenging students, understanding, 112–116
Chappell, Dave, 15
Charter schools
    operation, 74
    presence, 14, 44
    scores, 75
Children
    accountability, 132
    attention span, increase, 96
    fresh starts, 151
    joy/safety, 120
    mental health crisis (APA declaration),
        96
    neurodivergence/learning difference, 87
Circles
    types, 138
    usage/components, 81–82, 137–138
ClassDojo (app), 44, 69, 142
Classes, transitions (bookending), 138
Classism, battle, 3
Classroom
    asset-based practices, 91–92
    circles, components, 137–138
    communities

issues, discussion, 13
Equity work, 162
    anti-racism, interaction, 4–5
    joy, experience, 122–1223
    white people, involvement, 5–6
Escalated adults, impact, 43
Escalation
    place, 40
    responses, 50
    space, 22–23
    zone, 23
Expulsion, 54
    moratorium, 78
Extrinsic motivation tools, 139–140

F

Families
    characteristics, 15
    communication, 141–142
    communities, relationship, 116–118
    connections (deposits, analogy), 142–143
    contact plan, making, 142
    home visits, 142
    involvement, methods, 116
    stakeholder role, 116
    struggles, 95
    teacher frustrations, sharing, 143
Fear, usage, 44
Feedback, 65, 134
    behavior, equivalence, 51–52
    channels, 25
    loop, problems, 115
Four Pivots, The (Ginwright), 17
Frame of reference, 14–15
Franklin, Kirk, 135
Frustration, display, 41

G

Games/activities, student frame of reference
        (absence), 121
Genius Hour, 75

Ginwright, Shawn, 17, 94
Good habits, building, 129
Good-news reports, 141
Grade-level standards, academics focus, 107
Group activity, 138

H

Hammond, Zaretta, 94
Hard reset, 145
Harm
    occurrence, 25
    perpetuation, 5–6
    racism, harm, 6
    system, perpetuation, 42
    unaddressed harm, 153
    understanding, 80–81
Healing, 24–25
Heterogenous group, experience, 56
High-performing student, reputation
        (establishment), 17
Home lives, difficulty, 93
Home visits, 142
Human experience, fullness, 41
Humanizing practices, 78

I

Ideas, opposition, 26–28
Identity
    student exploration, 944
    understanding, 23
Identity politics, 31
Immigration challenges, 93
Implicit Association Tests (IAT), 19
Incarcerated people, 4th-grade reading level, 87
Individual actors/actions, hyper-focus, 90
Individual incentives, 139
Individualism, 90
Individualized Education Plans (IEPs), 58,
        108, 139, 162
    meaning, 65–67
Inequity, 34–36

Inquiry play, 74
Institutional racism, 85
Instruction
    discipline, impact, 79
    sit-and-get model, 36
    small-group instructions, 105
Instructional practices, building, 107
Intellectual legacy, 33
Intent, impact (contrast), 16–17
Interactions, 50
Interconnected relationships, 71
Interdependent ecosystem, creation, 109–112
Internal work, 18–19
Investment, focus, 130

J

Jones, Kenneth, 89
Joy
    appearance, 74
    earning, 61
    experience, 122–123
    focus, 39
    importance, 118–122
    moments, 59
    role, 57
    supply, 109
Judgment-free zone, 20

K

Kahoot, usage, 122
KKK violence, 88
Kleinfield, Judith, 94

L

Ladson-Billings, Gloria, 32
Language
    infraction, punishment, 80
    problems, 114
Leadership, problem, 25
Learning
    difference, 87

occurrence, 64
LGBTQ+ students, support, 31
Liberatory pedagogies, 91
Life lessons, transfer, 39
"Lost Instruction: The Disparate Impact of the School Discipline Gap in California," 79
Love, Bettina, 117
Low-stakes issues, energy (expenditure), 72

M

Make-up work (classroom procedure), 131
Management
    classroom management, 70–72
    extension, 68–82
    quality, defining, 69–70
Manipulatives, 74
Mann, Horace, 35–36
Meditation, incorporation, 138
Mental health, studies, 96
Mental stress, 73
Messaging, importance, 130
Microaggression, 832
Middle school, dynamics/challenges, 113
Mindful minute, usage, 138
Mindfulness, activities/usage, 138–139
Monitoring, policing (contrast), 73
Morale boosters, usage, 152–153
Morning meetings, 109
    components, 137–138
Morris, Monique, 87
"Most difficult" (shorthand), 67
Museum trips, usage, 118–119
Myers, Vernā, 134

N

Needs, communication (classroom procedure), 131
Neurodivergence, 87
Neurotypical, term (usage), 162
No Child Left Behind, 34